ABLAZE

ABLAZE
Igniting Young Minds

SEMESTER I & II

The Department of English
Auxilium College (Autonomous),
Vellore

B L O O M S B U R Y
NEW DELHI • LONDON • OXFORD • NEW YORK • SYDNEY

BLOOMSBURY INDIA
Bloomsbury Publishing India Pvt. Ltd
Second Floor, LSC Building No. 4, DDA Complex, Pocket C – 6 & 7,
Vasant Kunj, New Delhi 110070

BLOOMSBURY, BLOOMSBURY ACADEMIC INDIA and the Diana logo are trademarks of Bloomsbury Publishing Plc

First published in 2024
This edition published in 2024

ISBN: 978-93-61311-20-8
2 4 6 8 10 9 7 5 3

Printed in India by Gopsons Papers Pvt. Ltd., Noida

To find out more about our authors and books, visit www.bloomsbury.com and sign up for our newsletters

Contents

Foreword

A simple text unfolds itself through various poems, short stories, biographies and prose essays. The strength of the book lies in the TANSCHE syllabus which had been gathered together over time and experience of English Professors in the State of Tamil Nadu. In order to make a contribution from our end in Auxilium College, being an Autonomous Institution, the Faculty Members of the Department of English have initiated a creative gamut of engaging dialogue and eloquent description, word games and storylines, embarking on exercises of nostalgia, humour, history and reality.

The remarkable efforts and motivation of the teaching community can be seen in the linguistic experiments woven to enable the Taught to imbibe and reproduce the English Language with the desired effect. The Teacher has the added responsibility of consciously protecting the Student from the inadvertent misuse of AI.

We do not want our students to lose the art of generating grammatically correct English sentences of their own accord. Let not their minds become lethargic, so as to rely on artificial intelligence when language can be produced and perceived by the linguistic regions of the human brain like the Broca's area and the Wernick's area. I am apprehensive that these amazing parts of the human brain will soon become dysfunctional and never ever "shine in use". Needless to say, we seem to be losing the fine art of creative writing, while relying on AI to create a poem for us!

Poetry as we know, is that which arises from the depths of one's soul and is certainly not a conglomeration of words jostled together, ungrammatically in social media apps, in childish word play or rhyme by so-called presumptuous poets, who invade the reader's space. Worse still, if compiled by unnatural means. It is therefore feared that too much reading of a substandard thing can be grossly mistaken as the right thing!

It is absolutely indispensable that our students be given the right study aid material for valuable texts. Let us give them the pure joy of using the English Language and its amazing intricacies that can be learnt through challenging and productive exercises that have been included in this General English textbook "ABLAZE" In doing so, we pay a tribute to this glorious global language that we love; that we often hear commingled with our mother tongues, on every street corner and News channel; interwoven with our destiny in a Post-Colonial era which harbours either a silent or a vehement resistance now and then. But to the Thinking Individual, one realizes that English is a language we cannot easily do without!

May our students become proficient in the much sought after skills in English – Listening, Speaking, Reading and Writing, from their concentrated and conscious efforts that they are persuaded to experience in the English classroom!

Dr. Vernum Cecilia
Associate Professor and Head of English (Rtd.)
PG and Research Department of English
Auxilium College (Autonomous), Vellore

Preface

The book *Ablaze: Igniting Young Minds* is a foundational English Text book for the first-year undergraduate students. The book is a collection of poems, essays, short stories and biographies accompanied by up-to-date exercises, language study activities, sample templates to hone language skills and innovative ideas to improve communication skills. The wide range of activities will actively engage the learner to develop language skills. The activities aim to provide an opportunity to express creatively and freely their ideas.

The course has been designed to impart values for life, communication skills and employability skills with proficiency required for the 21st century learner to perform multiple tasks to progress and get ahead in career. The objective is to help the learner to acquire language skills essential in academic and real-life situations, to access information, interact, comprehend the content of texts for study and perform well in a job.

The activities of Semester I will enable the learner to express gratitude and apology, to pledge social responsibility, solve word puzzles, anagrams and identify the right words, to review a story, a book or a movie, to recall traditions of family, groups and society, to introduce oneself and others, chalk out daily schedule, to ask and give directions, write about a favourite sport and a commentary of a sports event, recall and write about a memorable day and a report of a cultural fest, describe a village/town or city, narrate travel experiences, analyze a biography, pick out favourite lines from a story, write about a role model, recall a challenging experience, enumerate achievements, plan for the future and writing to persuade.

The activities of Semester II will equip the learner to do a SWOC analysis, transform negative comments to positive affirmations, write letters and attempt a persuasive dialogue, express opinions and draft a resume, make a self-assessment, try narrative and creative writing, compare and contrast people and situations, learn problem solving skills, write a dialogue and to engage in group discussions, design posters and fill forms, sketch a family tree and complete a timeline and try reflective journal writing.

The onset of AI Assistants and Chatbots does not qualify the learner but makes them depend on such an easy way out than improve one's performance in academics and to prepare themselves for their advancement in Career. The language activities prescribed in the book *Ablaze: Igniting Young Minds* are meant to make the student learn and do the tasks assigned to them having acquired the necessary skills.

We gratefully acknowledge the contribution of the faculty of the department of English in designing the innovative exercises. The book *Ablaze: Igniting Young Minds* will prove to be a comprehensive source to the learner to take a leap as graduates from Classroom to boardroom.

Dr. (Sr.) Amala Valarmathy A.
Vice Principal
Associate Professor and Head of English
Auxilium College (Autonomous), Vellore

Contributors

Department of English
(Auxilium College, Autonomous, Gandhinagar, Vellore)

- **Dr. Hilda Princi Annie. S.** M.A, M.Phil, NET, PhD, Asst. Prof
- **Dr. Latha. E,** M.A, PhD, Asst. Prof
- **Dr. Geetha. R,** M.A, M.Phil, PhD, Asst. Prof & Head i/c (shift II)
- **Ms. Gayathri. R,** M.A, M.Phil, (PhD), Asst. Prof
- **Ms. Priyadharshni V.R,** M.A, (PhD), Asst. Prof
- **Ms. Anitha Daisy Winfred,** M.A, NET, (PhD), Asst. Prof
- **Ms. Janani. U,** M.A, M.Phil, NET, (PhD), Asst. Prof
- **Ms. Uthrra S,** M.A, M.Phil, Asst. Prof
- **Dr. Chitralekha. D,** M.A, M.Phil, SET, PhD, Asst. Prof
- **Ms. Griffa E.J,** M.A, NET, Asst. Prof
- **Ms. Starry Angeline D.** M.A, Asst. Prof
- **Dr. Sangamitra. B,** M.A, M.Phil, PhD, Asst. Prof
- **Dr. Kalpana Chatterjee,** M.A, M.Phil, PhD, Asst. Prof
- **Ms. Isvarya P,** M.A, M.Phil, NET, Asst. Prof
- **Dr. Janice Sandra David,** M.A, PhD, Asst. Prof
- **Dr. Caroline Unnatha Mani,** K. M.A, M.Phil, PhD, Asst. Prof
- **Dr. Nisha K.,** M.A, MSW, PhD, Asst. Prof
- **Ms. Aarthi G.,** M.A., PhD, Asst. Prof

SEMESTER I

I Am Malala

Malala Yousafzai

When I was born, people in our village commiserated with my mother and nobody congratulated my father. I arrived at dawn as the last star blinked out. We Pashtuns see this as an auspicious sign. My father didn't have any money for the hospital or for a midwife so a neighbour helped at my birth. My parents' first child was stillborn but I popped out kicking and screaming. I was a girl in a land where rifles are fired in celebration of a son, while daughters are hidden away behind a curtain, their role in life simply to prepare food and give birth to children.

For most Pashtuns it's a gloomy day when a daughter is born. My father's cousin Jehan Sher Khan Yousafzai was one of the few who came to celebrate my birth and even gave a handsome gift of money. Yet, he brought with him a vast family tree of our clan, the Dalokhel Yousafzai, going right back to my great-great-grandfather and showing only the male line. My father, Ziauddin, is different from most Pashtun men. He took the tree, drew a line like a lollipop from his name and at the end of it he wrote, 'Malala'. His cousin laughed in astonishment. My father didn't care. He says he looked into my eyes after I was born and fell in love. He told people, 'I know there is something different about this child.' He even asked friends to throw dried fruits, sweets and coins into my cradle, something we usually only do for boys.

I was named after Malalai of Maiwand, the greatest heroine of Afghanistan. Pashtuns are a proud people of many tribes split between Pakistan and Afghanistan. We live as we have for centuries by a code called *Pashtunwali*, which obliges us to give hospitality to all guests and in which the most important value is nang or honour. The worst thing that can happen to a Pashtun is loss of face. Shame is a very terrible thing for a Pashtun man. We have a saying, 'Without honour, the world counts for nothing.' We fight and feud among ourselves so much that our word for cousin – *tarbur* – is the same as our word for enemy. But we always come together against outsiders who try to conquer our lands. All Pashtun children grow up with the story of how Malalai inspired the Afghan army to defeat the British in 1880 in one of the biggest battles of the Second Anglo-Afghan War.

Malalai was the daughter of a shepherd in Maiwand, a small town on the dusty plains west of Kandahar. When she was a teenager, both her father and the man she was supposed to marry were among thousands of Afghans fighting against the British occupation of their country. Malalai went to the battlefield with other women from the village to tend the wounded and take them water. She saw their men were losing, and when the flag-bearer fell she lifted her white veil up high and marched onto the battlefield in front of the troops.

'Young love!' she shouted. 'If you do not fall in the battle of Maiwand then, by God, someone is saving you as a symbol of shame.'

Malalai was killed under fire, but her words and bravery inspired the men to turn the battle around. They destroyed an entire brigade, one of the worst defeats in the history of the British army. The Afghans were so proud that the last Afghan king built a Maiwand victory monument in the centre of Kabul. In high school I read some Sherlock Holmes and laughed to see that this was the same battle where Dr Watson was wounded before becoming partner to the great detective. In Malalai we Pashtuns have our very own Joan of Arc. Many girls' schools in Afghanistan are named after her. But my grandfather, who was a religious scholar and village cleric, didn't like my father giving me that name. 'It's a sad name,' he said. 'It means grief-stricken.'

When I was a baby my father used to sing me a song written by the famous poet Rahmat Shah Sayel of Peshawar. The last verse ends,

> O Malalai of Maiwand,
> Rise once more to make Pashtuns understand the song of honour,
> Your poetic words turn worlds around,
> I beg you, rise again

My father told the story of Malalai to anyone who came to our house. I loved hearing the story and the songs my father sang to me, and the way my name floated on the wind when people called it.

We lived in the most beautiful place in all the world. My valley, the Swat Valley, is a heavenly kingdom of mountains, gushing waterfalls and crystal-clear lakes. Welcome to Paradise, it says on a sign as you enter the valley. In olden times Swat was called Uddyana, which means 'garden'. We have fields of wild flowers, orchards of delicious fruit, emerald mines and rivers full of trout. People often call Swat the Switzerland of the East – we even had Pakistan's first ski resort. The rich people of Pakistan came on holiday to enjoy our clean air and scenery and our Sufi festivals of music and dancing. And so did many foreigners, all of whom we called *angrezan* – 'English' – wherever they came from. Even the Queen of England came, and stayed in the White Palace that was built from the same marble as the Taj Mahal by our king, the first wali of Swat.

We have a special history too. Today Swat is part of the province of Khyber Pakhtunkhwa, or KPK, as many Pakistanis call it, but Swat used to be separate from the rest of Pakistan. We were once a princely state, one of three with the neighbouring lands of Chitral and Dir. In colonial times our kings owed allegiance to the British but ruled their own land. When the British gave India independence in 1947 and divided it, we went with the newly created Pakistan but stayed autonomous. We used the Pakistani rupee, but the government of Pakistan could only intervene on foreign policy. The wali administered justice, kept the peace between warring tribes and collected *ushur* – a tax of ten per cent of income – with which he built roads, hospitals and schools.

We were only a hundred miles from Pakistan's capital Islamabad as the crow flies but it felt as if it was in another country. The journey took at least five hours by road over the Malakand Pass, a vast bowl of mountains where long ago our ancestors led by a preacher called Mullah Saidullah (known by the British as the Mad Fakir) battled British forces among the craggy peaks. Among them was Winston Churchill, who wrote a book about it, and we still call one of the peaks Churchill's Picket even though he was not very complimentary about our people. At the end of the pass is a green-domed shrine where people throw coins to give thanks for their safe arrival.

No one I knew had been to Islamabad. Before the troubles came, most people, like my mother, had never been outside Swat.

We lived in Mingora, the biggest town in the valley, in fact the only city. It used to be a small place but many people had moved in from surrounding villages, making it dirty and crowded. It has hotels, colleges, a golf course and a famous bazaar for buying our traditional embroidery, gemstones and anything you can think of. The Marghazar stream loops through it, milky brown from the plastic bags and rubbish thrown into it. It is not clear like the streams in the hilly areas or like the wide River Swat just outside town, where people fished for trout and which we visited on holidays. Our house was in Gulkada, which means 'place of flowers', but it used to be called Butkara, or 'place of the Buddhist statues'. Near our home was a field scattered with mysterious ruins – statues of lions on their haunches, broken columns, headless figures and, oddest of all, hundreds of stone umbrellas.

Islam came to our valley in the eleventh century when Sultan Mahmud of Ghazni invaded from Afghanistan and became our ruler, but in ancient times Swat was a Buddhist kingdom. The Buddhists had arrived here in the second century and their kings ruled the valley for more than 500 years. Chinese explorers wrote stories of how there were 1,400 Buddhist monasteries along the banks of the River Swat, and the magical sound of temple bells would ring out across the valley. The temples are long gone, but almost anywhere you go in Swat, amid all the primroses and other wild flowers, you find their remains. We would often picnic among rock carvings of a smiling fat Buddha sitting crosslegged on a lotus flower. There are many stories that Lord Buddha himself came here because it is a place of such peace, and some of his ashes are said to be buried in the valley in a giant stupa.

Our Butkara ruins were a magical place to play hide and seek. Once some foreign archaeologists arrived to do some work there and told us that in times gone by it was a place of pilgrimage, full of beautiful temples domed with gold where Buddhist kings lay buried. My father wrote a poem, 'The Relics of Butkara', which summed up perfectly how temple and mosque could exist side by side: 'When the voice of truth rises from the minarets,/ The Buddha smiles,/ And the broken chain of history reconnects.'

We lived in the shadow of the Hindu Kush mountains, where the men went to shoot ibex and golden cockerels. Our house was one storey and proper concrete. On the left were steps up to a flat roof big enough for us children to play cricket on. It was our playground. At dusk my father and his friends often gathered to sit and drink tea there. Sometimes I sat on the roof too, watching the smoke rise from the cooking fires all around and listening to the nightly racket of the crickets.

Our valley is full of fruit trees on which grow the sweetest figs and pomegranates and peaches, and in our garden we had grapes, guavas and persimmons. There was a plum tree in our front yard which gave the most delicious fruit. It was always a race between us and the birds to get to them. The birds loved that tree. Even the woodpeckers.

For as long as I can remember my mother has talked to birds. At the back of the house was a veranda where the women gathered. We knew what it was like to be hungry so my mother always cooked extra and gave food to poor families. If there was any left she fed it to the birds. In Pashto we love to sing *tapey*, two-line poems, and as she scattered the rice she would sing one: 'Don't kill doves in the garden./ You kill one and the others won't come.'

I liked to sit on the roof and watch the mountains and dream. The highest mountain of all is the pyramid-shaped Mount Elum. To us it's a sacred mountain and so high that it always wears a necklace of fleecy clouds. Even in summer it's frosted with snow. At school we learned that in 327 BC, even before the Buddhists came to Swat, Alexander the Great swept into the valley with thousands of elephants and soldiers on his way from Afghanistan to the Indus. The Swati people fled up the mountain, believing they would be protected by their gods because it was so high. But Alexander was a determined and patient leader. He built a wooden ramp from which his catapults and arrows could reach the top of the mountain. Then he climbed up so he could catch hold of the star of Jupiter as a symbol of his power.

From the rooftop I watched the mountains change with the seasons. In the autumn chill winds would come. In the winter everything was white snow, long icicles hanging from the roof like daggers, which we loved to snap off. We raced around, building snowmen and snow bears and trying to catch snowflakes. Spring was when Swat was at its greenest. Eucalyptus blossom blew into the house, coating everything white, and the wind carried the pungent smell of the rice fields. I was born in summer, which was perhaps why it was my favourite time of year, even though in Mingora summer was hot and dry and the stream stank where people dumped their garbage.

When I was born we were very poor. My father and a friend had founded their first school and we lived in a shabby shack of two rooms opposite the school. I slept with my mother and father in one room and the other was for guests. We had no bathroom or kitchen, and my mother cooked on a wood fire on the ground and washed our clothes at a tap in the school. Our home was always full of peoplevisiting from the village. Hospitality is an important part of Pashtun culture.

Two years after I was born my brother Khushal arrived. Like me he was born at home as we still could not afford the hospital, and he was named Khushal like my father's school, after the Pashtun hero Khushal Khan Khattak, a warrior who was also a poet. My mother had been waiting for a son and could not hide her joy when he was born. To me he seemed very thin and small, like a reed that could snap in the wind, but he was the apple of her eye, her *ladla*. It seemed to me that his every wish was her command. He wanted tea all the time, our traditional tea with milk and sugar and cardamom, but even my mother tired of this and eventually made some so bitter that he lost the taste for it. She wanted to buy a new cradle for him – when I was born my father couldn't afford one so they used an old wooden one from the neighbours which was already third or fourth hand – but my father refused. 'Malala swung in that cradle,' he said. 'So can he.' Then, nearly five years later, another boy was born – Atal, bright-eyed and inquisitive like a squirrel. After that, said my father, we were complete. Three children is a small family by Swati standards, where most people have seven or eight.

I played mostly with Khushal because he was just two years younger than me, but we fought all the time. He would go crying to my mother and I would go to my father. 'What's wrong, *Jani*?' he would ask. Like him I was born double-jointed and can bend my fingers right back on themselves. And my ankles click when I walk, which makes adults squirm.

My mother is very beautiful and my father adored her as if she were a fragile china vase, never laying a hand on her, unlike many of our men. Her name Tor Pekai means 'raven tresses' even though her hair is chestnut brown. My grandfather, Janser Khan, had been listening to Radio Afghanistan just before she was born and heard the name. I wished I had her white-lily skin, fine features and green eyes, but instead had inherited the sallow complexion, wide nose and brown eyes of my father. In our culture we all have nicknames – aside from *Pisho*, which my mother had called me since I was a baby, some of my cousins called me *Lachi*, which is Pashto for 'cardamom'. Black-skinned people are often called white and short people tall. We have a funny sense of humour. My father was known in the family as *Khaista dada*, which means beautiful.

When I was around four years old I asked my father, '*Aba*, what colour are you?' He replied, 'I don't know, a bit white, a bit black.'

'It's like when one mixes milk with tea,' I said.

He laughed a lot, but as a boy he had been so self-conscious about being dark-skinned that he went to the fields to get buffalo milk to spread on his face, thinking it would make him lighter. It was only when he met my mother that he became comfortable in his own skin. Being loved by such a beautiful girl gave him confidence.

In our society marriages are usually arranged by families, but theirs was a love match. I could listen endlessly to the story of how they met. They came from neighbouring villages in a remote valley in the upper Swat called Shangla and would see each other when my father went to his uncle's house to study, which was next door to that of my mother's aunt. They glimpsed enough of each other to know they liked one another, but for us it is taboo to express such things. Instead he sent her poems she could not read.

'I admired his mind,' she says.

'And me, her beauty,' he laughs.

There was one big problem. My two grandfathers did not get on. So when my father announced his desire to ask for the hand of my mother, Tor Pekai, it was clear neither side would welcome the marriage. His own father said it was up to him and agreed to send a barber as a messenger, which is the traditional way we Pashtuns do this. Malik Janser Khan refused the proposal, but my father is a stubborn man and persuaded my grandfather to send the barber again. Janser Khan's hujra was a gathering place for people to talk politics, and my father was often there, so they had got to know each other. He made him wait nine months but finally agreed.

My mother comes from a family of strong women as well as influential men. Her grandmother – my great-grandmother – was widowed when her children were young, and her eldest son Janser Khan was locked up because of a tribal feud with another family when he was only nine. To get him released she walked forty miles alone over mountains to appeal to a powerful cousin. I think my mother would do the same for us. Though she cannot read or write, my father shares everything with her, telling her about his day, the good and the bad. She teases him a lot and gives him advice about who she thinks is a genuine friend and who is not, and my father says she is always right. Most Pashtun men never do this, as sharing problems with women is seen as weak. 'He even asks his wife!' they say as an insult. I see my parents happy and laughing a lot. People would see us and say we are a sweet family.

My mother is very pious and prays five times a day, though not in the mosque as that is only for the men. She disapproves of dancing because she says God would not like it, but she loves to decorate herself with pretty things, embroidered clothes and golden necklaces and bangles. I think I am a bit of a disappointment to her as I am so like my father and don't bother with clothes and jewels. I get bored going to the bazaar but I love to dance behind closed doors with my school friends.

Growing up, we children spent most of our time with our mother. My father was out a lot as he was busy, not just with his school, but also with literary societies and *jirgas*, as well as trying to save the environment, trying to save our valley. My father came from a backward village yet through education and force of personality he made a good living for us and a name for himself.

People liked to hear him talk, and I loved the evenings when guests visited. We would sit on the floor around a long plastic sheet which my mother laid with food, and eat with our right hand as is our custom, balling together rice and meat. As darkness fell we sat by the light of oil lamps, batting away the flies as our silhouettes made dancing shadows on the walls. In the summer months there would often be thunder and lightning crashing outside and I would crawl closer to my father's knee.

I would listen rapt as he told stories of warring tribes, Pashtun leaders and saints, often through poems that he read in a melodious voice, crying sometimes as he read. Like most people in Swat we are from the Yousafzai tribe. We Yousafzai (which some people spell Yusufzai or Yousufzai) are originally from Kandahar and are one of the biggest Pashtun tribes, spread across Pakistan and Afghanistan.

Our ancestors came to Swat in the sixteenth century from Kabul, where they had helped a Timurid emperor win back his throne after his own tribe removed him. The emperor rewarded them with important positions in the court and army, but his friends and relatives warned him that the Yousafzai were becoming so powerful they would overthrow him. So one night he invited all the chiefs to a banquet and set his men on them while they were eating. Around 600 chiefs were massacred. Only two escaped, and they fled to Peshawar along with their tribesmen. After some time they went to visit some tribes in Swat to win their support so they could return to Afghanistan. But they were so captivated by the beauty of Swat they instead decided to stay there and forced the other tribes out.

The Yousafzai divided up all the land among the male members of the tribe. It was a peculiar system called *wesh* under which every five or ten years all the families would swap villages and redistribute the land of the new village among the men so that everyone had the chance to work on good as well as bad land. It was thought this would then keep rival clans from fighting. Villages were ruled by khans, and the common people, craftsmen and labourers, were their tenants. They had to pay them rent in kind, usually a share of their crop. They also had to help the khans form a militia by providing an armed man for every small plot of land. Each khan kept hundreds of armed men both for feuds and to raid and loot other villages.

As the Yousafzai in Swat had no ruler, there were constant feuds between the khans and even within their own families. Our men all have rifles, though these days they don't walk around with them like they do in other Pashtun areas, and my great-grandfather used to tell stories of gun battles when he was a boy. In the early part of the last century they became worried about being taken over by the British, who by then controlled most of the surrounding lands. They were also tired of the endless bloodshed. So they decided to try and find an impartial man to rule the whole area and resolve their disputes.

After a couple of rulers who did not work out, in 1917 the chiefs settled on a man called Miangul Abdul Wadood as their king. We know him affectionately as Badshah Sahib, and though he was completely illiterate, he managed to bring peace to the valley. Taking a rifle away from a Pashtun is like taking away his life, so he could not disarm the tribes. Instead he built forts on mountains all across Swat and created an army. He was recognised by the British as the head of state in 1926 and installed as wali, which is our word for ruler. He set up the first telephone system and built the first primary school and ended the *wesh* system because the constant moving between villages meant no one could sell land or had any incentive to build better houses or plant fruit trees.

In 1949, two years after the creation of Pakistan, he abdicated in favour of his elder son Miangul Abdul Haq Jehanzeb. My father always says, 'While Badshah Sahib brought peace, his son brought prosperity.' We think of Jehanzeb's reign as a golden period in our history. He had studied in a British school in Peshawar, and perhaps because his own father was illiterate he was passionate about schools and built many, as well as hospitals and roads. In the 1950s he ended the system where people paid taxes to the khans. But there was no freedom of expression, and if anyone criticised the wali, they could be expelled from the valley. In 1969, the year my father was born, the wali gave up power and we became part of Pakistan's North-West Frontier Province, which a few years ago changed its name to Khyber Pakhtunkhwa.

So I was born a proud daughter of Pakistan, though like all Swatis I thought of myself first as Swati and then Pashtun, before Pakistani.

Near us on our street there was a family with a girl my age called Safina and two boys similar in age to my brothers, Babar and Basit. We all played cricket on the street or rooftops together, but I knew as we got older the girls would be expected to stay inside. We'd be expected to cook and serve our brothers and fathers. While boys and men could roam freely about town, my mother and I could not go out without a male relative to accompany us, even if it was a five-year-old boy! This was the tradition.

I had decided very early I would not be like that. My father always said, 'Malala will be free as a bird.' I dreamed of going to the top of Mount Elum like Alexander the Great to touch Jupiter and even beyond the valley. But, as I watched my brothers running across the roof, flying their kites and skilfully flicking the strings back and forth to cut each other's down, I wondered how free a daughter could ever be.

Exercise

"I was a girl in a land where rifles are fired in celebration of a son, while daughters are hidden away behind a curtain, their role in life simply to prepare food and give birth to children."

The memoir of Malala is the story of a brave girl who survived the brutal attack as she stood up for the right to education of every child and won the Nobel Peace Prize in 2014. Her life story instils confidence and pride in being born a woman.

A. Self-Introduction

Points to remember:

- Start with your name
- Be Confident
- Be Concise
- Have a professional tone
- Highlight your details
- End with a strong statement
- Smile and make eye contact

Introduce Yourself
• Hi, my name's Sarah.
• I'm from India.
• I'm a Doctor.
• I work for CNR hospital.
• My father is a lawyer and my mother a homemaker.
• My hobby is painting.
• My favorite sport is Tennis.
• I speak three languages.
• I like cooking. I cook continental foods.
• I like reading books.
• My favorite place is Taj Mahal.
• I Study English because it's a global language.

Introduce Yourself
• Hi, my name's ______
• I'm from ______
• I'm a ______
• I work for ______
• My father is a ______ and my mother ______.
• My hobby is ______.
• My favorite sport is ______.
• I speak ______.
• I like ______. I ______.
• I like ______.
• My favorite place is ______.
• I Study English because ______.

B. Introducing people

Points to remember:

- Start with a greeting
- Provide the context of for how you met your friend
- Highlight her interests and talents
- Share a personal trait that showcases her personality
- Express enthusiasm for others to meet her

> Hey everyone, I'd like to introduce my friend, Riya! We met in dance class last year and quickly became close friends. Riya is a skilled dancer and also a singer. She's also passionate about environmental activism.. She's always up for an adventure and has a contagious laugh. I'm so glad you're finally meeting her!"

> Hey everyone, I ______
> ______
> ______
> ______
> ______
> ______

C. Solve the Crossword Puzzle below:

ACROSS

2. Malala was awarded the Nobel prize for ________
5. The School Malala has studied ________
6. The Nationality of Malala ________
8. The Islamic fundamental group in Afghanistan ________
9. A City in swat district ________

DOWN

1. The System of swapping a village every 10 years and redistributing lands among the villagers
3. Malala's area of activism
4. A Prominent Afghan poet
7. An Ethnic group of Afghanistan and Pakistan

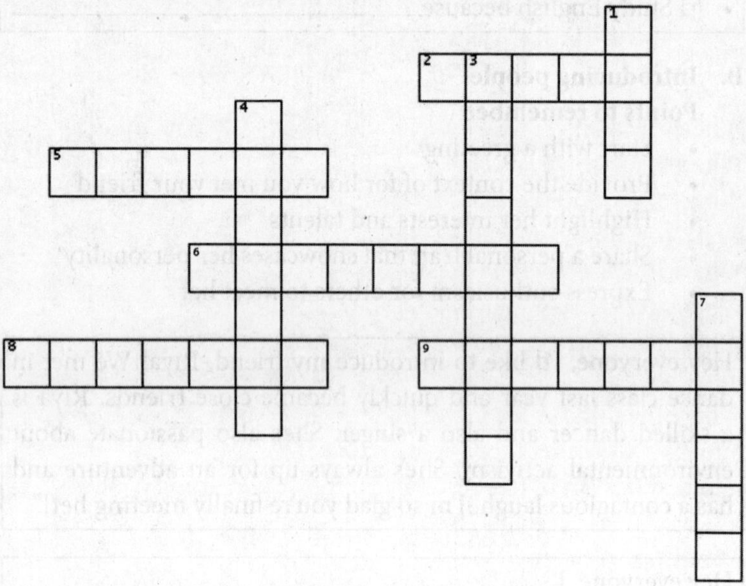

Where the Mind is Without Fear

Rabindranath Tagore

Where the mind is without fear and the head is held high
Where knowledge is free
Where the world has not been broken up into fragments
By narrow domestic walls
Where words come out from the depth of truth
Where tireless striving stretches its arms towards perfection
Where the clear stream of reason has not lost its way
Into the dreary desert sand of dead habit
Where the mind is led forward by thee
Into ever-widening thought and action
Into that heaven of freedom, my Father, let my country awake.

Exercise

**"...into that heaven of freedom, my father,
let my country awake"**

The poem was written when India was still under the colonial rule of the British. The poet envisions a new India that is free from the clutches of evil and superstitious practices. He exhorts the people to be open-minded, sincere, and hardworking and to keep away from all discriminatory practices.

A. Paraphrase a poem of your choice with the cues given below:

(a) Read the following lines at your pace
(b) Re-read the lines to note out words that are new to you
(c) Try to get the contextual meaning with the aid of your dictionary and rewording **(Paraphrasing by Synonyms)**
(d) Read it again with the substituted equivalent words **(Direct Paraphrasing)**
(e) Retell the poem in your own words without changing the meaning **(Indirect Paraphrasing)**
(f) Briefly narrate the meaning of the verse **(Summary Paraphrasing)**
(g) Try to change the sentence structure to frame number of grammatically correct sentences by preserving the actual sense of the content **(Transformational Paraphrasing)**
(h) Use a similar context to better explain the sense **(Adaptation Paraphrasing)**

Let's Ponder the Poem

B. As you read the captivating verses, take time to reflect and enhance these imaginative lines with your own thoughts.

Poet:	
Title/Alternative Title:	
What is the poem about (Theme)?	What is the message the author is conveying?

- Is there one line that communicates the poem's theme or argument? Write it below:

- What aspects of the poem did you find enjoyable, what did you learn, and what was challenging to understand?

- What do you know about the speaker in the poem?

- Doodle & Describe any imagery/setting or conflict in the poem

Difficult words/meanings

Poetic Devices

- Does the poet use particular words to evoke images or feelings in the reader?

- Share your thoughts on the poem. Explain its significance in a few sentences, as if you were discussing it with a friend?

The School for Sympathy

E.V. Lucas

Part 1: Narrator's Visit to the School of Sympathy

I had heard a lot about Miss Beam's School, but I did not get the chance to visit it till last week. When I arrived at the school, I saw a girl of about twelve with her eyes covered with a bandage being led carefully between the flowerbeds by a little boy of eight. She stopped and asked who it was that had come in and he seemed to be describing me to her. Then they passed on.

Miss Beam was all that I had expected - middle-aged, authoritative, kind and understanding. Her hair was beginning to turn grey, and her round figure was likely to be comforting to a homesick child.

We chatted for a while, and when I asked her some questions about her teaching methods, which I had heard were simple, she said:

'...We teach only those things that are simple and useful to pupils- spelling, adding, subtracting, multiplying, writing, etc. The rest is done by reading to them and giving them interesting tasks. There are practically no other lessons.'

'... I have heard so much,' I said, 'about the originality of your system.' Miss Beam smiled. 'Ah, yes,' she said. 'I am coming to that.'

'The real aim of this school is not to teach thought but thoughtfulness, humanity, kindness and citizenship. That is the ideal I have always had, and happily there are parents good enough to trust me to try and put it into practice. Look out of the window a minute, will you?'

I went to the window, which looked out on a large garden and playground at the back What do you see?' Miss Beam asked.

'I see some very beautiful grounds,' I said, 'and a lot of jolly children. But what surprises me, and pains me too, is that they are not at all healthy and active. As I came in I saw one poor little thing being led about because of some trouble with her eyes. And now I can see two more in the same condition, while there is a girl with a crutch just under the window watching the others at play. She seems to be a hopeless cripple.'

Miss Beam laughed.

'Oh, no,' she said, 'She is not lame really; this is only her lame day. Nor are those others blind, it is only their blind day.'

I must have looked very much astonished, for she laughed again.

Miss Beam's Account of Her School

'There you have an essential part of our system in a nutshell. In order to get these young minds to appreciate and understand misfortune, we make them share in misfortune too. In the course of the term every child has one blind day, one lame day, one deaf day and one dumb day. During the blind day their eyes are bandaged, and it is a point of honour not to peep. The bandage is put on overnight, they wake up blind. This means that they need assistance in everything, and other children are told to help them and lead them about. It is educative to both of them - the blind and the helpers.'

'Everyone is very kind,' Miss Beam continued, 'and it is really something of a joke, although, of course, before the day is over the reality of the disability becomes clear even to the least thoughtful. The blind day is, of course, really the worst, but some of the children tell me that the dumb day is the most frightening. There, of course, the child must use will-power only because the mouth is not bandaged... But come down into the garden and see for yourself how the children like it.'

Narrator's Experience in the School for Sympathy

'Here's a gentleman come to talk to you,' said Miss Beam, and left us. 'Don't you ever peep?' I asked, by way of an opening.

'Oh, no,' she exclaimed, 'that would be cheating! But I had no idea it was so awful to be blind. You can't see a thing. One feels one is going to be hit by something every moment. Sitting down is such a relief.'

Are your guides kind to you? I asked.

'Pretty good. Not as careful as I shall be when it is my turn. Those that have been Blind already are the best. It is terrible not to see. I wish you would try.' 'Shall I lead you anywhere?' I asked.

'Oh, yes,' she said, 'let's go for a little walk. Only you must tell me about things. I shall be so glad when today's over. The other bad days can't be half as bad as this. Having a leg tied up and hopping about on a crutch is almost a fun, I guess. Having an arm tied up is a little more troublesome, because you have to get your food cut up for you, and so on, but it doesn't really matter. And as for being deaf for a day, I shan't mind that – at least, not much. But being blind is so frightening. My head aches all the time, just from avoiding things that probably aren't there. Where are we now?' 'In the playground,' I said, 'going towards the house.'

Miss Beam is walking up and down the terrace with a tall girl.

'What has the girl got on?' My companion asked me. 'A blue skirt and a pink blouse.'

'I think it's Millie,' she said. 'What colour is her hair?' 'Very light,' I said.

'Yes, that's Millie. She is the head girl. She is very decent.' 'There's an old man tying up roses,' I said.

'Yes, that's Peter. He is the gardener. He's hundreds of years old!' 'And here comes a dark girl in red, on crutches.' 'Yes,' she said, 'that's Berryl.'

And so we walked on, and in guiding this little girl about I discovered that I was many times more thoughtful already than usual. I also realised that having to describe the surroundings to another, makes them more interesting.

When Miss Beam came to release me I was sorry to go. I walked back to the town murmuring (incorrectly as ever) the lines: Can I see another's woe, And not share their sorrow too? O no, never can it be,

Never, never, can it be.

Exercise

"The real aim of this school is not to teach thought but thoughtfulness, humanity, kindness and citizenship."

The story unfolds with the narrator describing his visit to an extraordinary school that imparts appreciation for life and thoughtfulness but the children have to learn it the hard way by having to experience days such as a blind day, a deaf day, or a lame day. The narrator emerges more transformed from his encounter with children who are more open and cooperative to learn through the innovative method.

The most cherished of all memories are that of school days as they were filled with loads of learning with fun and laughter.

A. Write about the most memorable day of your school.

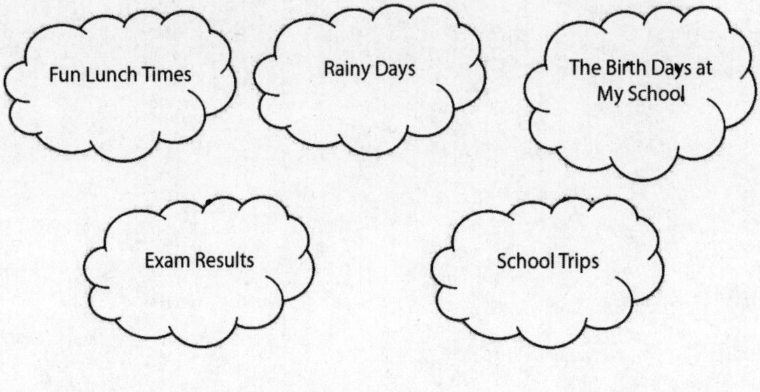

B. Write a Report for your College Magazine describing the Cultural Fest held at your college.

The Donkey

G.K. Chesterton

When fishes flew and forests walked
    And figs grew upon thorn,
Some moment when the moon was blood
    Then surely I was born.

With monstrous head and sickening cry
    And ears like errant wings,
The devil's walking parody
    On all four-footed things.

The tattered outlaw of the earth,
    Of ancient crooked will;
Starve, scourge, deride me: I am dumb,
    I keep my secret still.

Fools! For I also had my hour;
    One far fierce hour and sweet:
There was a shout about my ears,
        And palms before my feet.over him.

Exercise

"For I also had my hour"

The poem begins with the self-hatred of the donkey describing itself as monstrous and ugly. When Christ rode him into Jerusalem triumphantly on Palm Sunday before his crucifixion, it is then that he realizes his self-worth.

Everyone has a special moment to shine, but in the meantime, one must focus on developing one's own personality and purpose. Answer the "self-discovery" questions below to learn more about yourself and become a better person.

1. What do you enjoy doing?

   ____

   ____

   ____

2. What are your strengths?

   ____

   ____

   ____

3. Write the statement of purpose (of your life)

   ____

   ____

   ____

4. How closely is your life aligned to your statement of purpose right now, rate yourself between 1 to 10?

   ____

   ____

   ____

5. What actions should you take to align yourself to live according to the statement of purpose? List it below

   - ______________________________
   - ______________________________
   - ______________________________
   - ______________________________

Complete the following sentences about you:

1. I feel happy when I ______________________________

   ____

   ____

2. I am proud of myself ______________________________
____
____
____

3. People often thank me for ___________________________
____
____
____

4. I can make a difference in the society by ______________
____
____
____

5. I can make my classroom a better place by ____________
____
____
____

6. I can learn better when I ___________________________
____
____
____

7. A short term goal of mine is _______________________
____
____

8. The long term goal of mine is ______________________
____
____
____

9. I should improve ______________________________
____
____
______________ to achieve these goals.

10. The value that I would highly uphold is ______________
____
______________________. Because it can change the world by
____

The Magic Brocade

A Tale of China

Once in China there lived an old widow and her son, Chen. The widow was known all over for the brocades that she made on her loom. Weaving threads of silver, gold, and colored silk into her cloth, she made pictures of flowers, birds, and animals, so real they seemed almost alive. People said there were no brocades finer than the ones the widow wove.

One day, the widow took a pile of brocades to the marketplace, where she quickly sold them. Then she went about buying her household needs.

All at once she stopped. "Oh, my!"

Her eye had been caught by a beautiful painted scroll that hung in one of the stalls. It showed a marvelous palace, all red and yellow and blue and green, reaching delicately to the sky. All around were fantastic gardens, and walking through them, the loveliest maidens.

"Do you like it?" asked the stall keeper. "It's a painting of Sun Palace. They say it lies far to the east and is the home of many fairy ladies."

"It's wonderful," said the widow with a shiver and a sigh. "It makes me want to be there."

Though it cost most of her money, the widow could not resist buying the scroll. When she got back to her cottage, she showed it to her son.

"Look, Chen. Have you ever seen anything more beautiful? How I would love to live in that palace, or at least visit it!"

Chen looked at her thoughtfully. "Mother, why don't you weave the picture as a brocade? That would be almost like being there."

"Why, Chen, what a marvelous idea! I'll start at once."

She set up her loom and began to weave. She worked for hours, then days, then weeks, barely stopping to eat or sleep. Her eyes grew bloodshot, and her fingers raw.

"Mother," said Chen anxiously, "shouldn't you get more rest?"

"Oh, Chen, it's so hard to stop. While I weave, I feel like I'm there at Sun Palace. And I don't want to come away!"

Because the widow no longer wove brocades to sell, Chen cut firewood and sold that instead. Months went by, while inch by inch the pattern appeared on the loom.

One day, Chen came in to find the loom empty and the widow sobbing. "What's wrong, Mother?" he asked in alarm.

She looked at him tearfully. "I finished it."

The brocade was laid out on the floor. And there it all was—the palace reaching to the sky, the beautiful gardens, the lovely fairy ladies.

"It looks so real," said Chen in amazement. "I feel like I could step into it!"

Just then, a sudden wind whipped through the cottage. It lifted the brocade, blew it out the window, and carried it through the air. The widow and her son rushed outside, only to watch the brocade disappear into the east.

"It's gone!" cried the widow, and she fainted away.

Chen carried her to her bed and sat beside her for many hours. At last her eyes opened.

"Chen," she said weakly, "you must find the brocade and bring it back. I cannot live without it."

"Don't worry, Mother. I'll go at once."

Chen gathered a few things and started to the east. He walked for hours, then days, then weeks. But there was no sign of the brocade.

One day, Chen came upon a lonely hut. Sitting by the door was an old, leather-skinned woman smoking a pipe. A horse was grazing nearby.

"Hello, deary," said the woman. "What brings you so far from home?"

"I'm looking for my mother's brocade. The wind carried it to the east."

"Ah, yes," said the woman. "The brocade of Sun Palace! Well, that wind was sent by the fairy ladies of the palace itself. They're using the brocade as a pattern for their weaving."

"But my mother will die without it!"

"Well, then, you had best get it back! But you won't get to Sun Palace by foot, so you'd better ride my horse. It will show you the way."

"Thank you!" said Chen.

"Oh, don't thank me yet, deary. Between here and there, you must pass through the flames of Fiery Mountain. If you make a single sound of complaint, you'll be burnt to ashes. After that, you must cross the Icy Sea. The smallest word of discontent, and you'll be frozen solid. Do you still want to go?"

"I must get back my mother's brocade."

"Good boy. Take the horse and go."

Chen climbed on, and the horse broke into a gallop. Before long they came to a mountain all on fire. Without missing a step, the horse started up the slope, leaping through the flames. Chen felt the fire singe his skin, but he bit his lip and made not a sound.

At last they came down the other side. When they'd left the flames behind, Chen was surprised to find that his burns were gone.

A little later, they came to a sea filled with great chunks of ice. Without pausing a moment, the horse began leaping from one ice floe to another. Waves showered them with icy spray, so that Chen was soaked and shivering. But he held his tongue and said not a word.

Finally they reached the far shore. At once, Chen felt himself dry and warm.

It wasn't long then till they came to Sun Palace. It looked just like his mother's brocade!

He rode to the entrance, sprang from the horse, and hurried into a huge hall. Sitting there at looms were dozens of fairy ladies, who turned to stare at him, then whispered to each other excitedly. On each loom was a copy of his mother's brocade, and the brocade itself hung in the center of the room.

A lady near the door rose from her loom to meet him. "My name is Lien, and I welcome you. You are the first mortal ever to reach our palace. What good fortune brings you here?"

The fairy was so beautiful that for a moment Chen could only stare. Lien gazed shyly downward.

"Dear lady, I have come for my mother's brocade."

"So you are the widow's son!" said Lien. "How we admire that brocade! None of us has been able to match it. We wish to keep it here till we can."

"But I must bring it home, or my mother will die!"

Lien looked alarmed, and a flurry of whispers arose in the room. She stepped away to speak softly with several others, then returned to Chen.

"We surely must not let that happen to her. Only let us keep the brocade for the rest of the day, so we can try to finish our own. Tomorrow you may take it back with you."

"Thank you, dear lady," said Chen.

The fairies worked busily to finish their brocades. Chen sat near Lien at her loom. As she wove, he told her about his life in the human world, and she told him about hers at Sun Palace. Many smiles and glances passed between them.

When darkness fell, the fairies worked on by the light of a magic pearl. At last Chen's eyes would stay open no longer, and he drifted to sleep on his chair.

One by one the fairies finished or left off, and went out of the hall. Lien was the last one there, and it was almost dawn when she was done. She cut her brocade from the loom and held it beside the widow's.

She sighed. "Mine is good, but the widow's is still better. If only she could come and teach us herself."

Then Lien had an idea. With needle and thread, she embroidered a small image onto the widow's brocade—an image of herself on the palace steps. She softly said a spell. Then she left the hall, with a last long smiling gaze at Chen.

When Chen woke up, the sun was just rising. He looked around the hall for Lien, but saw no one. Though he longed to find her to say goodbye, he told himself, "I must not waste a moment."

He rolled up his mother's brocade, rushed from the hall, and jumped onto the horse. Back he raced, across the Icy Sea and over Fiery Mountain.

When he reached the old woman's hut, she was standing there waiting for him. "Hurry, Chen! Your mother is dying! Put on these shoes, or you'll never get there in time."

Chen put them on. One step, two, three, then he was racing over the countryside faster than he could believe possible. In no time, he was home.

He rushed into the cottage and found the widow in bed, pale and quiet. "Mother!"

Her eyes opened slowly. "Chen?"

"Mother, I brought it." He unrolled the cloth onto the bed.

"My brocade!" The widow raised herself to look. Color came back to her face, and she seemed already stronger.

"Chen, I need more light. Let's take it outside."

He helped her out of the cottage and placed the brocade on a rock. But just then a sudden wind came, and the brocade rose slowly in the air. It stretched as it rose, growing larger and larger, till it filled their view completely. The palace was as large as Chen himself had seen it, and standing on the steps was the fairy lady Lien.

Lien was beckoning with her hand. "Quickly!" she called. "While the wind still blows! Step into the brocade!"

For a moment, Chen was too astounded to move. Then he took hold of his mother's arm, and together they stepped forward. There was a shimmering, and there they stood before Sun Palace.

Lien rushed up to them, and the other fairies gathered around. She said to the widow, "Welcome, honored one. If it pleases you, we wish you to live with us and teach us the secrets of your craft."

"Nothing could please me more!" cried the widow. "But, Chen, is it all right with you?"

Chen looked in Lien's eyes and smiled. "Yes, Mother, it's just fine with me."

So the widow became teacher to the fairies, and Chen became husband to Lien. And people say there are no brocades finer than the ones they weave at Sun Palace.

EXERCISE

"The widow was known all over for the brocades that she made on her loom. Weaving threads of silver, gold, and coloured silk into her cloth, she made pictures of flowers, birds, and animals, so real they seemed almost alive."

The story celebrates the unparalleled love of a mother and her selfless sacrifice. She becomes obsessed with weaving a beautiful landscape and the brocade is carried away by a mysterious wind to the fairies of the Sun palace and she is heartbroken at the loss of it. The son vows to recover it at the cost of his life for the love of his mother and is duly rewarded for his courage, sacrifice, and devotion to his mother.

A. Think about a challenging experience you have faced and brainstorm how those experiences can help someone to achieve their goals.

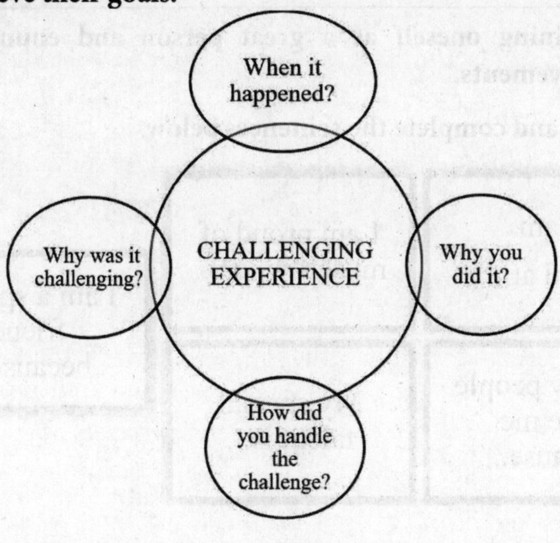

"I did it when I was in university. I had to be away from my family for the first time. At the age of eighteen, I had not yet begun the new semester and had hardly any friends. I missed my family and friends a lot. But I had faith in my ability to adapt to new surroundings and people. To overcome loneliness, I looked for some interesting activities. I became a member of the English-speaking club. In addition, I went to Malaysia for a student exchange program. Through these experiences, I made a lot of wonderful friends and developed into a more sociable and active person. I thought it was a challenging experience because I'll overcome it, just like I did before."

- I did it when I was …

  ____

  ____

- I did it because / to show/to make…

  ____

  ____

- I handled this challenge by…

  ____

  ____

- I thought it was challenging because …

  ____

  ____

B. Imagining oneself as a great person and enumerating achievements.

Read and complete the sentences below.

I am good at...	I am proud of myself when...	I am a special friend because...
I know people like me because...	My special talent is...	

The Story of My Experiments with Truth

M.K. Gandhi

Birth and Parentage

The Gandhis belong to the Bania caste and seem to have been originally grocers. But for three generations, from my grandfather, they have been Prime Ministers in several Kathiawad States. Uttamchand Gandhi, alias Ota Gandhi, my grandfather, must have been a man of principle. State intrigues compelled him to leave Porbandar, where he was Diwan, and to seek refuge in Junagadh. There he saluted the Nawab with the left hand. Someone, noticing the apparent discourtesy, asked for an explanation, which was given thus: 'The right hand is already pledged to Porbandar.' Ota Gandhi married a second time, having lost his first wife. He had four sons by his first wife and two by his second wife. I do not think that in my childhood I ever felt or knew that these sons of Ota Gandhi were not all of the same mother. The fifth of these six brothers was Karamchand Gandhi, alias Kaba Gandhi, and the sixth was Tulsidas Gandhi. Both these brothers were Prime Ministers in Porbandar, one after the other. Kaba Gandhi was my father. He was a member of the Rajasthanik Court. It is now extinct, but in those days it was a very influential body for settling disputes between the chiefs and their fellow clansmen. He was for some time Prime Minister in Rajkot and then in Vankaner. He was a pensioner of the Rajkot State when he died. Kaba Gandhi married four times in succession, having lost his wife each time by death. He had two daughters by his first and second marriages. His last wife, Putlibai, bore him a daughter and three sons, I being the youngest. My father was a lover of his clan, truthful, brave and generous, but short-tempered. To a certain extent he might have been even given to carnal pleasures. For he married for the fourth time when he was over forty. But he was incorruptible and had earned a name for strict impartiality in his family as well as outside. His loyalty to the State was well known. An Assistant Political Agent spoke insultingly of the Rajkot Thakore Saheb, his chief, and he stood up to the insult. The Agent was angry and asked Kaba Gandhi to apologize. This he refused to do and was therefore kept under detention for a few hours. But when the Agent saw that Kaba Gandhi was adamant, he ordered him to be released. My father never had any ambition to accumulate riches and left us very little property. He had no education, save that of experience. At best, he might be said to have read up to the fifth Gujarati standard. Of history and geography he was innocent. But his rich experience of practical affairs stood him in good stead in the solution of the most intricate questions and in managing hundreds of men. Of religious training he had very little, but he had that kind of religious culture which frequent visits to temples and listening to religious discourses make available to many Hindus. In his last days he began reading the Gita at the instance of a learned Brahman friend of the family, and he used to repeat aloud some verses every day at the time of worship. The outstanding impression my mother has left on my memory is that of saintliness. She was deeply religious. She would not think of taking her meals without her daily prayers. Going to Haveli-the Vaishnava temple-was one of her daily duties. As far as my memory can go back, I do not remember her having ever missed the Chaturmas1 . She would take the hardest vows and keep them without flinching. Illness was no excuse for relaxing them. I can recall her once falling ill when she was observing the Chandrayana2 vow, but the illness was not allowed to interrupt the observance. To keep two or three consecutive fasts was nothing to her. Living on one meal a day during Chaturmas was a habit with her. Not content with that, she fasted every alternate day during one Chaturmas. During another Chaturmas she vowed not to have food without seeing the sun. We children on those days would stand, staring at the sky, waiting to announce the appearance of the sun to our mother. Everyone knows that at the height of the rainy season the sun often does not condescend to show his face. And I remember days when, at his sudden appearance, we would rush and announce it to her. She would run out to see with her own eyes, but by that time the fugitive sun would be gone, thus depriving her of her meal. "That does not matter;" she would say cheerfully, "God did not want me to eat today." And then she would return to her round of duties. My mother had strong common sense. She was well informed about all matters of State, and ladies of the court thought highly of her intelligence. Often I would accompany her, exercising the privilege of childhood, and I still remember many lively discussions she had with the widowed mother of the Thakore Saheb. Of these parents I was born at Porbandar, otherwise known as Sudamapuri, on the 2nd October, 1869. I passed my childhood in Porbandar. I recollect having been put to school. It was with some difficulty that I got through the multiplication tables. The fact that I recollect nothing more of those days than having learnt, in company with other boys, to call our teacher all kinds of names, would strongly suggest that my intellect must have been sluggish, and my memory raw.

Childhood

I must have been about seven when my father left Porbandar for Rajkot to become a member of the Rajasthanik Court. There I was put into a primary school, and I can well recollect those days, including the names and other particulars of the teachers who taught me. As at Porbandar, so here, there is hardly anything to note about my studies. I could only have been a mediocre student. From this school I went to the suburban school and thence to the high school, having already reached my twelfth year. I do not remember having ever told a lie, during this short period, either to my teachers or to my schoolmates. I used to be very shy and avoided all company. My books and my lessons were my sole companions. To be at school at the stroke of the hour and to run back home as soon as the school closed–that was my daily habit. I literally ran back, because I could not bear to talk to anybody. I was even afraid lest anyone should poke fun at me. There is an incident which occurred at the examination during my first year at the high school and which is worth recording. Mr. Giles, the Educational Inspector, had come on a visit of inspection. He had set us five words to write as a spelling exercise. One of the words was 'kettle'. I had mis-spelt it. The teacher tried to prompt me with the point of his boot, but I would not be prompted. It was beyond me to see that he wanted me to copy the spelling from my neighbour's slate, for I had thought that the teacher was there to supervise us against copying. The result was that all the boys, except myself, were found to have spelt every word correctly. Only I had been stupid. The teacher tried later to bring this stupidity home to me, but without effect. I never could learn the art of 'copying'. Yet the incident did not in the least diminish my respect for my teacher. I was, by nature, blind to the faults of elders. Later I came to know of many other failings of this teacher, but my regard for him remained the same. For I had learnt to carry out the orders of elders, not to scan their actions. Two other incidents belonging to the same period, have always clung to my memory. As a rule I had a distaste for any reading beyond my school books. The daily lessons had to be done, because I disliked being taken to task by my teacher as much as I disliked deceiving him. Therefore I would do the lessons, but often without my mind in them. Thus when even the lessons could not be done properly, there was of course no question of any extra reading. But somehow my eyes fell on a book purchased by my father. It was Shravana Pitribhakti Nataka (a play about Sharavana's devotion to his parents). I read it with intense interest. There came to our place about the same time itinerant showmen. One of the pictures I was shown was of Shravana carrying, by means of slings fitted for his shoulders, his blind parents on a pilgrimage. The book and the picture left an indelible impression on my mind. 'Here is an example for you to copy,' I said to myself. The agonized lament of the parents over Shravana's death is still fresh in my memory. The melting tune moved me deeply, and I played it on a concertina which my father had purchased for me. There was a similar incident connected with another play. Just about this time, I had secured my father's permission to see a play performed by a certain dramatic company. This play-Harishchandra-captured my heart. I could never be tired of seeing it. But how often should I be permitted to go? It haunted me and I must have acted Harishchandra to myself times without number. 'Why should not all be truthful like Harishchandra?' was the question I asked myself day and night. To follow truth and to go through all the ordeals Harishchandra went through was the one ideal it inspired in me. I literally believed in the story of Harishchandra. The thought of it all often made me weep. My common sense tells me today that Harishchandra could not have been a historical character. Still both Harishchandra and Shravana are living realities for me, and I am sure I should be moved as before if I were to read those plays again today.

Child Marriage

Much as I wish that I had not to write this chapter, I know that I shall have to swallow many such bitter draughts in the course of this narrative. And I cannot do otherwise, if I claim to be a worshipper of Truth. It is my painful duty to have to record here my marriage at the age of thirteen. As I see the youngsters of the same age about me who are under my care, and think of my own marriage, I am inclined to pity myself and to congratulate them on having escaped my lot. I can see no moral argument in support of such a preposterously early marriage. Let the reader make no mistake. I was married, not betrothed. For in Kathiawad there are two distinct rites – betrothal and marriage. Betrothal is a preliminary promise on the part of the parents of the boy and the girl to join them in marriage, and it is not inviolable. The death of the boy entails no widowhood on the girl. It is an agreement purely between the parents, and the children have no concern with it. Often they are not even informed of it. It appears that I was betrothed thrice, though without my knowledge. I was told that two girls chosen for me had died in turn, and therefore I infer that I was betrothed three times. I have a faint recollection, however, that the third betrothal took place in my seventh year. But I do not recollect having been informed about it. In the present chapter I am talking about my marriage, of which I have the clearest recollection. It will be remembered that we were three brothers. The first was already married. The elders decided to marry my second brother, who was two or three years my senior, a cousin, possibly a year older, and me, all at the same time. In doing so there was no thought of our welfare, much less our wishes. It was purely a question of their own convenience and economy. Marriage among Hindus is no simple matter. The parents of the bride and the bridegroom often bring themselves to ruin over it. They waste their substance, they waste their time. Months are taken up over the preparations – in making clothes and ornaments and in preparing budgets for dinners. Each tries to outdo the other in the number and variety of courses to be prepared. Women, whether they have a voice or no, sing themselves hoarse, even get ill, and disturb the peace of their neighbours. These in their turn quietly put up with all the turmoil and bustle, all the dirt and filth, representing the remains of the feasts, because they know that a time will come when they also will be behaving in the same manner. It would be better, thought my elders, to have all this bother over at one and the same time. Less expense and greater éclat. For money could be freely spent if it had only to be spent once instead of thrice. My father and my uncle were both old, and we were the last children they had to marry. It is likely that they wanted to have the last best time of their lives. In view of all these considerations, a triple wedding was decided upon, and as I have said before, months were taken up in preparation for it. It was only through these preparations that we got warning of the coming event. I do not think it meant to me anything more than the prospect of good clothes to wear, drum beating, marriage processions, rich dinners and a strange girl to play with. The carnal desire came later. I propose to draw the curtain over my shame, except for a few details worth recording. To these I shall come later. But even they have little to do with the central idea I have kept before me in writing this story. So my brother and I were both taken to Porbandar from Rajkot. There are some amusing details of the preliminaries to the final drama – e.g., smearing our bodies all over with turmeric paste – but I must omit them. My father was a Diwan, but nevertheless a servant, and all the more so because he was in favour with the Thakore Saheb. The latter would not let him go until the last moment. And when he did so, he ordered for my father special stage coaches, reducing the journey by two days. But the fates had willed otherwise. Porbandar is 120 miles from Rajkot – a cart journey of five days. My father did the distance in three, but the coach toppled over in the third stage, and he sustained severe injuries. He arrived bandaged all over. Both his and our interest in the coming event was half destroyed, but the ceremony had to be gone through. For how could the marriage dates be changed? However, I forgot my grief over my father's injuries in the childish amusement of the wedding. I was devoted to my parents. But no less was I devoted to the passions that flesh is heir to. I had yet to learn that all happiness and pleasure should be sacrificed in devoted service to my parents. And yet, as though by way of punishment for my desire for pleasures, an incident happened, which has ever since rankled in my mind and which I will relate later. Nishkulanand sings: 'Renunciation of objects, without the renunciation of desires, is short-lived, however hard you may try'. Whenever I sing this song or hear it sung, this bitter untoward incident rushes to my memory and fills me with shame. My father put on a brave face in spite of his injuries, and took full part in the wedding. As I think of it, I can even today call before my mind's eye the places where he sat as he went through the different details of the ceremony. Little did I dream then that one day I should severely criticize my father for having married me as a child. Everything on that day seemed to me right and proper and pleasing. There was also my own eagerness to get married. And as everything that my father did then struck me as beyond reproach, the recollection of those things fresh in my memory. I can picture to myself, even today, how we sat on our wedding dais, how we performed the Saptapadi1 , how we, the newly wedded husband and wife, put the sweet Kansar2 into each other's mouth, and how we began to live together. And oh! that first night. Two innocent children all unwittingly hurled themselves into the ocean of life. My brother's wife had thoroughly coached me about my behaviour on the first night. I do not know who had coached my wife. I have never asked her about it, nor am I inclined to do so now. The reader may be sure that we were too nervous to face each other. We were certainly too shy. How was I to talk to her, and what was I to say? The coaching could not carry me far. But no coaching is really necessary in such matters. The impressions of the former birth are potent enough to make all coaching superfluous. We gradually began to know each other, and to speak freely together. We were the same age. But I took no time in assuming the authority of a husband.

Exercise

"The book and the picture left an indelible impression on my mind. 'Here is an example for you to copy,' I said to myself."

The extract chronicles the early life of the Father of our nation and it is a critical account of oneself and renders a glimpse of a great soul and his upbringing in a household that valued inclusiveness simultaneously adhering to the social and cultural customs of the time.

"Autobiographies are only useful as the lives you read about and analyze may suggest to you something that you may find useful in your own journey through life," says Eleanor Roosevelt.

A. Analysing a Biography: Based on your understanding let's skim through the biography and be nourished

- Summary of the Chapter ______________________________
____
____
____
____
____

- Purpose of the Chapter ____________________

____

____

____

____

- Structure ____________________

____

____

____

____

- Style ____________________

____

____

____

____

- Segment Topics ____________________

____

____

____

____

Divide the chapter into segments and give appropriate subheading.

1. ____________	5. ____________
2. ____________	6. ____________
3. ____________	7. ____________
4. ____________	8. ____________

B. Pick out your favourite lines; state how those lines inspired you.

- " ____________________

____

____

____

____________________"

- " ____________________

____

____

____

___________________________"

C. Writing about your role model or a person you admire the most.

1. The person I admire the most is ____________
2. He/she is my ____________________
3. The quality I admire the most about him/her is that ______
____
4. He/she always helps me with my ____________
5. He/she also helps my parents with __________
6. When he/she helps others selflessly, they feel very happy and
____
7. He/she is also a very brave and ____________
8. He/she is never scared of anything, and ________
9. He/she always says that instead of getting scared, we must
____
10. I admire his/her spirit of sacrifice and __________

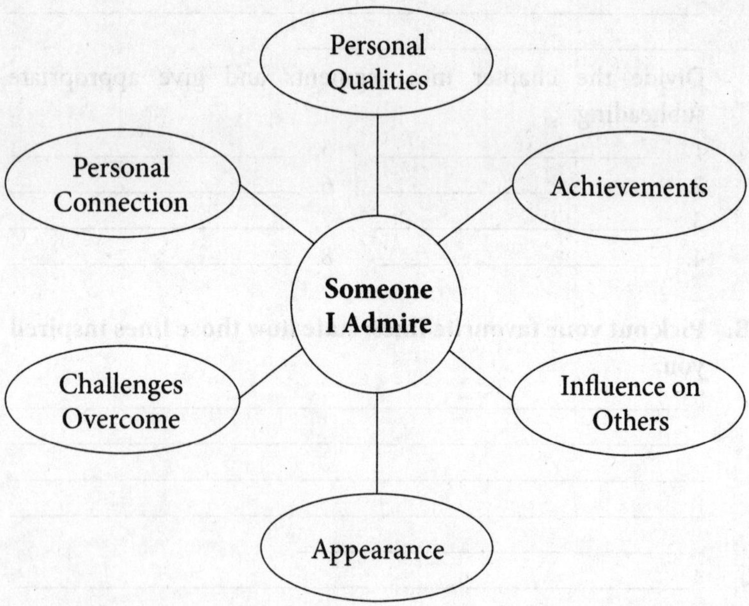

Nine Gold Medals

David Roth

The athletes had come from all over the country
To run for the gold, for the silver and bronze
Many weeks and months of training
All coming down to these games.

The spectators gathered around the old field
To cheer on all the young women and men
The final event of the day was approaching
Excitement grew high to begin.

The blocks were all lined up for those who would use them
The hundred-yard dash and the race to be run
These were nine resolved athletes in back of the starting line
Poised for the sound of the gun.

The signal was given, the pistol exploded
And so did the runners all charging ahead
But the smallest among them, he stumbled and staggered
And fell to the asphalt instead.

He gave out a cry in frustration and anguish
His dreams and his efforts all dashed in the dirt
But as sure as I'm standing here telling this story
The same goes for what next occurred.

The eight other runners pulled up on their heels
The ones who had trained for so long to compete
One by one they all turned around and went back to help him
And brought the young boy to his feet.

Then all nine runners joined hands and continued
The one hundred metres reduced to a walk
And the banner above that said (Special Olympics)
Could not have been more on the mark.

That's how the race ended, with nine gold medals
They came to the finish line holding hands still
And a standing ovation And nine beaming faces
Said more than these words ever will.

Exercise

> **"The athletes had come from all over the country**
> **To run for the gold, for the silver and bronze"**

The poem is based on a true event that happened during the special Olympics in 1976 track and field event for the differently abled, when one of the contestants stumbled on the asphalt and a few others turned around and went back to help him and linked arms together and walked together to the finish line.

A. Write a passage about your favourite Sport using the vocabulary given below:

Physical, Entertainment, To develop, To sharpen, Stress, To ameliorate

B. Let's imagine it's a thrilling sports day event – 100 meters Dash. Write the commentary for a sports event of your choice using the format given below:

"Good morning, sports fans, and welcome to an electrifying day of athletic excellence here at the Annual Sports Day Extravaganza! I'm your commentator, [Your Name], and we've got a packed schedule today with events that promise to keep you on the edge of your seat.

First up, the 100-meter dash! The runners are lined up at the starting blocks. Right now; all eyes are on the track as we gear up for the marquee event of the day—the 100 meters Dash. The atmosphere is absolutely buzzing with excitement as the athletes take their positions at the starting line. You can feel the tension in the air as the competitors focus intently on the track ahead.

And there's the starting pistol! They're off! Exploding out of the blocks, the sprinters are giving it everything they've got. It's a blur of speed and power as they surge down the track. The crowd is on their feet, roaring with anticipation!

Look at Lane 4! That's [Athlete's Name], pulling ahead with an incredible burst of acceleration. But wait, Lane 6 is closing the gap! It's going to be a photo finish—every second counts!

And as they cross the finish line, it's a spectacular race! The winner is [Athlete's Name] by the slimmest of margins—what an incredible display of speed and determination. The crowd is going wild, and we've just witnessed a truly memorable 100 meters Dash. Stay tuned, sports fans—there's plenty more excitement to come!

The Things that Haven't Been Done Before

Edgar Albert Guest

The things that haven't been done before,
Those are the things to try;
Columbus dreamed of an unknown shore
At the rim of the far-flung sky,
And his heart was bold and his faith was strong
As he ventured in dangers new,
And he paid no heed to the jeering throng
Or the fears of the doubting crew.

The many will follow the beaten track
With guideposts on the way.
They live and have lived for ages back
With a chart for every day.
Someone has told them it's safe to go
On the road he has traveled o'er,
And all that they ever strive to know
Are the things that were known before.

A few strike out without map or chart,
Where never a man has been,
From the beaten path they draw apart
To see what no man has seen.
There are deeds they hunger alone to do;
Though battered and bruised and sore,
They blaze the path for the many, who
Do nothing not done before.

The things that haven't been done before
Are the tasks worthwhile today;
Are you one of the flock that follows, or
Are you one that shall lead the way?
Are you one of the timid souls that quail
At the jeers of a doubting crew,
Or dare you, whether you win or fail,
Strike out for a goal that's new?

Exercise

"The things that haven't been done before
Are the tasks worthwhile today."

The poem is built on the example of Christopher Colombus, the master navigator who is known for his exploration of the Americas. The poet endeavours to motivate people to take risks and to be innovative, breaking free from the beaten track and mapping unchartered territories.

A. Planning for the future

Talk about your dream achievement using the following words:

Wish, would like to see myself, dream of, will be, would have become

1. I want to see myself working as an Assistant Professor.
2. I wish to hold the position of Managing Director of a company

3. I will be working as a Chartered Accountant.
4. I dream to ____________________
5. I would have become ____________________

B. Persuasive Writing

- Persuasive writing is about convincing the reader to adopt a certain viewpoint, take specific action, or agree with the writer's argument.
- It involves presenting logical arguments, appealing to emotions, and providing reliable information to influence the reader's perspective.

The primary goal is to persuade the reader to align with the author's standpoint.

S Suitable topic/title
T Tell reasons for support or oppose
A Add supporting facts
G Give evidence
E Ending

To Remember:
- Establish a Clear Position
- Use Logical Arguments and Evidence
- Appeal to Emotions and Values

Task: Is social media beneficial or detrimental? Discuss.

The Ugly Duckling

Hans Christian Andersen

The haystacks piled up in the meadows looked beautiful. The stork walking about on his long red legs chattered in the Egyptian language, which he had learnt from his mother. The corn-fields and meadows were surrounded by large forests, in the midst of which were deep pools. It was, indeed, delightful to walk about in the country. In a sunny spot stood a pleasant old farm-house close by a deep river, and from the house down to the water side grew great burdock leaves, so high, that under the tallest of them a little child could stand upright. The spot was as wild as the centre of a thick wood. In this snug retreat sat a duck on her nest, watching for her young brood to hatch; she was beginning to get tired of her task, for the little ones were a long time coming out of their shells, and she seldom had any visitors. The other ducks liked much better to swim about in the river than to climb the slippery banks, and sit under a burdock leaf, to have a gossip with her. At length one shell cracked, and then another, and from each egg came a living creature that lifted its head and cried, 'Peep, peep.' 'Quack, quack,' said the mother, and then they all quacked as well as they could, and looked about them on every side at the large green leaves. Their mother allowed them to look as much as they liked, because green is good for the eyes. 'How large the world is,' said the young ducks, when they found how much more room they now had than while they were inside the egg-shell. 'Do you imagine this is the whole world?' asked the mother; 'Wait till you have seen the garden; it stretches far beyond that to the parson's field, but I have never ventured to such a distance. Are you all out?' she continued, rising; 'No, I declare, the largest egg lies there still. I wonder how long this is to last, I am quite tired of it;' and she seated herself again on the nest.

'Well, how are you getting on?' asked an old duck, who paid her a visit.

'One egg is not hatched yet,' said the duck, 'it will not break. But just look at all the others, are they not the prettiest little ducklings you ever saw? They are the image of their father, who is so unkind, he never comes to see.'

'Let me see the egg that will not break,' said the duck; 'I have no doubt it is a turkey's egg. I was persuaded to hatch some once, and after all my care and trouble with the young ones, they were afraid of the water. I quacked and clucked, but all to no purpose. I could not get them to venture in. Let me look at the egg. Yes, that is a turkey's egg; take my advice, leave it where it is and teach the other children to swim.'

'I think I will sit on it a little while longer,' said the duck; 'as I have sat so long already, a few days will be nothing.'

'Please yourself,' said the old duck, and she went away.

At last the large egg broke, and a young one crept forth crying, 'Peep, peep.' It was very large and ugly. The duck stared at it and exclaimed, 'It is very large and not at all like the others. I wonder if it really is a turkey. We shall soon find it out, however when we go to the water. It must go in, if I have to push it myself.'

On the next day the weather was delightful, and the sun shone brightly on the green burdock leaves, so the mother duck took her young brood down to the water, and jumped in with a splash. 'Quack, quack,' cried she, and one after another the little ducklings jumped in. The water closed over their heads, but they came up again in an instant, and swam about quite prettily with their legs paddling under them as easily as possible, and the ugly duckling was also in the water swimming with them.

'Oh,' said the mother, 'that is not a turkey; how well he uses his legs, and how upright he holds himself! He is my own child, and he is not so very ugly after all if you look at him properly. Quack, quack! come with me now, I will take you into grand society, and introduce you to the farmyard, but you must keep close to me or you may be trodden upon; and, above all, beware of the cat.'

When they reached the farmyard, there was a great disturbance, two families were fighting for an eel's head, which, after all, was carried off by the cat. 'See, children, that is the way of the world,' said the mother duck, whetting her beak, for she would have liked the eel's head herself. 'Come, now, use your legs, and let me see how well you can behave. You must bow your heads prettily to that old duck yonder; she is the highest born of them all, and has Spanish blood, therefore, she is well off. Don't you see she has a red flag tied to her leg, which is something very grand, and a great honour for a duck; it shows that everyone is anxious not to lose her, as she can be recognized both by man and beast. Come, now, don't turn your toes, a well-bred duckling spreads his feet wide apart, just like his father and mother, in this way; now bend your neck, and say "quack".'

The ducklings did as they were bid, but the other duck stared, and said, 'Look, here comes another brood, as if there were not enough of us already! and what a queer looking object one of them is; we don't want him here,' and then one flew out and bit him in the neck.

'Let him alone,' said the mother; 'he is not doing any harm.'

'Yes, but he is so big and ugly,' said the spiteful duck 'and therefore he must be turned out.'

'The others are very pretty children,' said the old duck, with the rag on her leg, 'all but that one; I wish his mother could improve him a little.'

'That is impossible, your grace,' replied the mother; 'he is not pretty; but he has a very good disposition, and swims as well or even better than the others. I think he will grow up pretty, and perhaps be smaller; he has remained too long in the egg, and therefore his figure is not properly formed;' and then she stroked his neck and smoothed the feathers, saying, 'It is a drake, and therefore not of so much consequence. I think he will grow up strong, and able to take care of himself.'

'The other ducklings are graceful enough,' said the old duck. 'Now make yourself at home, and if you can find an eel's head, you can bring it to me.'

And so they made themselves comfortable; but the poor duckling, who had crept out of his shell last of all, and looked so ugly, was bitten and pushed and made fun of, not only by the ducks, but by all the poultry. 'He is too big,' they all said, and the turkey cock, who had been born into the world with spurs, and fancied himself really an emperor, puffed himself out like a vessel in full sail, and flew at the duckling, and became quite red in the head with passion, so that the poor little thing did not know where to go, and was quite miserable because he was so ugly and laughed at by the whole farmyard. So it went on from day to day till it got worse and worse. The poor duckling was driven about by everyone; even his brothers and sisters were unkind to him, and would say, 'Ah, you ugly creature, I wish the cat would get you,' and his mother said she wished he had never been born. The ducks pecked him, the chickens beat him, and the girl who fed the poultry kicked him with her feet. So, at last he ran away, frightening the little birds in the hedge as he flew over the palings.

'They are afraid of me because I am ugly,' he said. So, he closed his eyes, and flew still farther, until he came out on a large moor, inhabited by wild ducks. Here he remained the whole night, feeling very tired and sorrowful.

In the morning, when the wild ducks rose in the air, they stared at their new comrade. 'What sort of a duck are you?' they all said, coming round him.

He bowed to them, and was as polite as he could be, but he did not reply to their question. 'You are exceedingly ugly,' said the wild ducks, 'but that will not matter if you do not want to marry one of our family.'

Poor thing! he had no thoughts of marriage; all he wanted was permission to lie among the rushes, and drink some of the water on the moor. After he had been on the moor two days, there came two wild geese, or rather goslings, for they had not been out of the egg long, and were very saucy. 'Listen, friend,' said one of them to the duckling, 'you are so ugly, that we like you very well. Will you go with us, and become a bird of passage? Not far from here is another moor, in which there are some pretty wild geese, all unmarried. It is a chance for you to get a wife; you may be lucky, ugly as you are.' 'Pop, pop,' sounded in the air, and the two wild geese fell dead among the rushes, and the water was tinged with blood. 'Pop, pop,' echoed far and wide in the distance, and whole flocks of wild geese rose up from the rushes. The sound continued from every direction, for the sportsmen surrounded the moor, and some were even seated on branches of trees, overlooking the rushes. The blue smoke from the guns rose like clouds over the dark trees, and as it floated away across the water, a number of sporting dogs bounded in among the rushes, which bent beneath them wherever they went. How they terrified the poor duckling! He turned away his head to hide it under his wing, and at the same moment a large terrible dog passed quite near him. His jaws were open, his tongue hung from his mouth, and his eyes glared fearfully. He thrust his nose close to the duckling, showing his sharp teeth, and then, 'splash, splash,' he went into the water without touching him, 'Oh,' sighed the duckling, 'how thankful I am for being so ugly; even a dog will not bite me.' And so he lay quite still, while the shot rattled through the rushes, and gun after gun was fired over him. It was late in the day before all became quiet, but even then, the poor young thing did not dare to move. He waited quietly for several hours, and then, after looking carefully around him, hastened away from the moor as fast as he could. He ran over field and meadow till a storm arose, and he could hardly struggle against it. Towards evening, he reached a poor little cottage that seemed ready to fall, and only remained standing because it could not decide on which side to fall first. The storm continued so violent, that the duckling could go no farther; he sat down by the cottage, and then he noticed that the door was not quite closed in consequence of one of the hinges having given way. There was therefore a narrow opening near the bottom large enough for him to slip through, which he did very quietly, and got a shelter for the night. A woman, a tom cat, and a hen lived in this cottage. The tom cat, whom the mistress called, 'My little son,' was a great favourite; he could raise his back, and purr, and could even throw out sparks from his fur if it were stroked the wrong way. The hen had very short legs, so she was called 'Chickie short legs.' She laid good eggs, and her mistress loved her as if she had been her own child. In the morning, the strange visitor was discovered, and the tom cat began to purr, and the hen to cluck.

'What is that noise about?' said the old woman, looking round the room, but her sight was not very good; therefore, when she saw the duckling, she thought it must be a fat duck, that had strayed from home. 'Oh, what a prize!' she exclaimed, 'I hope it is not a drake, for then I shall have some duck's eggs. I must wait and see.' So, the duckling was allowed to remain on trial for three weeks, but there were no eggs. Now the tom cat was the master of the house, and the hen was mistress, and they always said, 'We and the world,' for they believed themselves to be half the world, and the better half too. The duckling thought that others might hold a different opinion on the subject, but the hen would not listen to such doubts. 'Can you lay eggs?' she asked. 'No.' 'Then have the goodness to hold your tongue.' 'Can you raise your back, or purr, or throw out sparks?' said the tom cat. 'No.' 'Then you have no right to express an opinion when sensible people are speaking.' So the duckling sat in a corner, feeling very low spirited, till the sunshine and the fresh air came into the room through the open door, and then he began to feel such a great longing for a swim on the water, that he could not help telling the hen.

'What an absurd idea,' said the hen. 'You have nothing else to do, therefore you have foolish fancies. If you could purr or lay eggs, they would pass away.'

'But it is so delightful to swim about on the water,' said the duckling, 'and so refreshing to feel it close over your head, while you dive down to the bottom. ''Delightful, indeed!' said the hen, 'why you must be crazy! Ask the cat, he is the cleverest animal I know, ask him how he would like to swim about on the water, or to dive under it, for I will not speak of my own opinion; ask our mistress, the old woman—there is no one in the world more clever than she is. Do you think she would like to swim, or to let the water close over her head?' 'You don't understand me,' said the duckling.

'We don't understand you? Who can understand you, I wonder? Do you consider yourself more clever than the cat, or the old woman? I will say nothing of myself. Don't imagine such nonsense, child, and thank your good fortune that you have been received here. Are you not in a warm room, and in society from which you may learn something? But you are a chatterer, and your company is not very agreeable. Believe me, I speak only for your own good. I may tell you unpleasant truths, but that is a proof of my friendship. I advise you, therefore, to lay eggs, and learn to purr as quickly as possible.' 'I believe I must go out into the world again,' said the duckling. 'Yes, do,' said the hen. So, the duckling left the cottage, and soon found water on which it could swim and dive, but was avoided by all other animals, because of its ugly appearance. Autumn came, and the leaves in the forest turned to orange and gold. then, as winter approached, the wind caught them as they fell and whirled them in the cold air. The clouds, heavy with hail and snow-flakes, hung low in the sky, and the raven stood on the ferns crying, 'Croak, croak.' It made one shiver with cold to look at him. All this was very sad for the poor little duckling. One evening, just as the sun set amid radiant clouds, there came a large flock of beautiful birds out of the bushes. The duckling had never seen any like them before. They were swans, and they curved their graceful necks, while their soft plumage shown with dazzling whiteness. They uttered a singular cry, as they spread their glorious wings and flew away from those cold regions to warmer countries across the sea. As they mounted higher and higher in the air, the ugly little duckling felt quite a strange sensation as he watched them. He whirled himself in the water like a wheel, stretched out his neck towards them, and uttered a cry so strange that it frightened himself. Could he ever forget those beautiful, happy birds; and when at last they were out of his sight, he dived under the water, and rose again almost beside himself with excitement. He knew not the names of these birds, nor where they had flown, but he felt towards them as he had never felt for any other bird in the world. He was not envious of these beautiful creatures, but wished to be as lovely as they. Poor ugly creature, how gladly he would have lived even with the ducks had they only given him encouragement. The winter grew colder and colder; he was obliged to swim about on the water to keep it from freezing, but every night the space on which he swam became smaller and smaller. At length it froze so hard that the ice in the water crackled as he moved, and the duckling had to paddle with his legs as well as he could, to keep the space from closing up. He became exhausted at last, and lay still and helpless, frozen fast in the ice.

Early in the morning, a peasant, who was passing by, saw what had happened. He broke the ice in pieces with his wooden shoe, and carried the duckling home to his wife. The warmth revived the poor little creature; but when the children wanted to play with him, the duckling thought they would do him some harm; so, he started up in terror, fluttered into the milk-pan, and splashed the milk about the room. Then the woman clapped her hands, which frightened him still more. He flew first into the butter-cask, then into the meal-tub, and out again. What a condition he was in! The woman screamed, and struck at him with the tongs; the children laughed and screamed, and tumbled over each other, in their efforts to catch him; but luckily he escaped. The door stood open; the poor creature could just manage to slip out among the bushes, and lie down quite exhausted in the newly fallen snow.

It would be very sad, were I to relate all the misery and privations which the poor little duckling endured during the hard winter; but when it had passed, he found himself lying one morning in a moor, amongst the rushes. He felt the warm sun shining, and heard the lark singing, and saw that all around was beautiful spring. Then the young bird felt that his wings were strong, as he flapped them against his sides, and rose high into the air. They bore him onwards, until he found himself in a large garden, before he well knew how it had happened. The apple-trees were in full blossom, and the fragrant elders bent their long green branches down to the stream which wound round a smooth lawn. Everything looked beautiful, in the freshness of early spring. From a thicket close by came three beautiful white swans, rustling their feathers, and swimming lightly over the smooth water. The duckling remembered the lovely birds, and felt more strangely unhappy than ever.

'I will fly to those royal birds,' he exclaimed, 'and they will kill me, because I am so ugly, and dare to approach them; but it does not matter: better be killed by them than pecked by the ducks, beaten by the hens, pushed about by the maiden who feeds the poultry, or starved with hunger in the winter.'

Then he flew to the water, and swam towards the beautiful swans. The moment they espied the stranger, they rushed to meet him with outstretched wings.

'Kill me,' said the poor bird; and he bent his head down to the surface of the water, and awaited death.

But what did he see in the clear stream below? His own image; no longer a dark, gray bird, ugly and disagreeable to look at, but a graceful and beautiful swan. To be born in a duck's nest, in a farmyard, is of no consequence to a bird, if it is hatched from a swan's egg. He now felt glad at having suffered sorrow and trouble, because it enabled him to enjoy so much better all the pleasure and happiness around him; for the great swans swam round the new-comer, and stroked his neck with their beaks, as a welcome.

Into the garden presently came some little children, and threw bread and cake into the water.

'See,' cried the youngest, 'there is a new one;' and the rest were delighted, and ran to their father and mother, dancing and clapping their hands, and shouting joyously, 'There is another swan come; a new one has arrived.'

Then they threw more bread and cake into the water, and said, 'The new one is the most beautiful of all; he is so young and pretty.' And the old swans bowed their heads before him.

Then he felt quite ashamed, and hid his head under his wing; for he did not know what to do, he was so happy, and yet not at all proud. He had been persecuted and despised for his ugliness, and now he heard them say he was the most beautiful of all the birds. Even the elder-tree bent down its bows into the water before him, and the sun shone warm and bright. Then he rustled his feathers, curved his slender neck, and cried joyfully, from the depths of his heart, 'I never dreamed of such happiness as this, while I was an ugly duckling.'

Exercise

"He had been persecuted and despised for his ugliness, and now he heard them say he was the most beautiful of all the birds."

The story of the Ugly Duckling is often interpreted as a metaphor for self-discovery, personal transformation, and the importance of acceptance, despite differences in appearance or perceived flaws. It teaches that true beauty and worth are not solely determined by outward appearance and that one should not judge others based on superficial characteristics. The 'ugly duckling' ultimately represents the idea that everyone has their own unique journey and that finding one's place in the world is often a process of self-discovery and acceptance.

A. Write the story map of the short story *The Ugly Duckling* that includes:

(a) Setting
(b) Characters
(c) Problem
(d) Solution

B. Reorder the sentences given below from the story in the correct sequence:

1. One big, ugly duckling came out.
2. He saw a beautiful white bird! 'Wow!' he said. 'Who's that?'
3. Mummy Duck lived on a farm.
4. No one wanted to be his friend.
5. You're a beautiful swan, like me.
6. It started to get cold. It started to snow!
7. In her nest, she had five little eggs and one big egg.
8. Do you want to be my friend?'
9. Five pretty, yellow baby ducklings came out.
10. Then spring came.

Alice Fell, Or Poverty

William Wordsworth

THE post-boy drove with fierce career,
For threatening clouds the moon had drowned;
When, as we hurried on, my ear
Was smitten with a startling sound.

As if the wind blew many ways,
I heard the sound,—and more and more;
It seemed to follow with the chaise,
And still I heard it as before.

At length I to the boy called out;
He stopped his horses at the word,
But neither cry, nor voice, nor shout,
Nor aught else like it, could be heard.

The boy then smacked his whip, and fast
The horses scampered through the rain;
But, hearing soon upon the blast
The cry, I bade him halt again.

Forthwith alighting on the ground,
"Whence comes," said I, "this piteous moan?"

And there a little Girl I found,
Sitting behind the chaise, alone.

"My cloak!" no other word she spake,
But loud and bitterly she wept,
As if her innocent heart would break;
And down from off her seat she leapt.

"What ails you, child?"—she sobbed "Look here!"
I saw it in the wheel entangled,
A weather-beaten rag as e'er
From any garden scare-crow dangled.

There, twisted between nave and spoke,
It hung, nor could at once be freed;
But our joint pains unloosed the cloak,
A miserable rag indeed!

"And whither are you going, child,
To-night alone these lonesome ways?"
"To Durham," answered she, half wild—
"Then come with me into the chaise."

Insensible to all relief
Sat the poor girl, and forth did send
Sob after sob, as if her grief
Could never, never have an end.

"My child, in Durham do you dwell?"
She checked herself in her distress,
And said, "My name is Alice Fell;
I'm fatherless and motherless.

"And I to Durham, Sir, belong."
Again, as if the thought would choke
Her very heart, her grief grew strong;
And all was for her tattered cloak!

The chaise drove on; our journey's end
Was nigh; and, sitting by my side,
As if she had lost her only friend
She wept, nor would be pacified.

Up to the tavern-door we post;
Of Alice and her grief I told;
And I gave money to the host,
To buy a new cloak for the old.

"And let it be of duffil grey,
As warm a cloak as man can sell!"
Proud creature was she the next day,
The little orphan, Alice Fell!

Exercise

"And said, "My name is Alice Fell;
I'm fatherless and motherless."

The poem is about the predicament of an orphan girl doomed to live in poverty and emphasizes the need to respond with compassion to the sufferings of fellow human beings. It calls forth to act on behalf of the less privileged and to extend acts of kindness to alleviate their adversities.

A. Read the pledge given below on Empowerment of Marginalized Society and prepare a pledge on anyone of the Sustainable Development Goals

I pledge to listen to the voices of the Marginalized Communities I promise to contribute towards social change by promoting education I promise that I will not discriminate anyone who is different from me I pledge to lend a helping hand to the suffering and needy people I promise to uphold justice and defend the helpless victims

B. Word Puzzle

Find out the words from the poem

R	A	E	B	A	L	O	N	E
E	D	L	S	O	B	C	E	P
L	F	I	G	R	I	E	F	I
I	H	T	G	P	A	I	S	T
E	T	T	S	H	N	G	M	E
F	C	L	O	A	K	M	A	O
X	V	E	L	N	E	W	C	U
S	M	I	T	T	E	N	K	S

1. A____
2. R_____
3. S____
4. S__
5. O_____
6. G____
7. R__
8. C____
9. P______
10. S______

C. Solve the anagrams/Write the correct words

1. udolc_____
2. dosun_____
3. oomn____
4. earecrtu________
5. ohsut_____
6. nniecotn________
7. dnarge______
8. hrsose______
9. ckhoe_____
10. veratn______

Three Sideway Stories from Wayside School by Louis Sachar

Aaron Shepard

NARRATOR 1: We're going to tell you about three of the children in Mrs. Jewls's class, on the thirtieth story of Wayside School.

NARRATOR 4: But before we get to them, there is something you ought to know. Wayside School was accidentally built sideways.

NARRATOR 2: It was supposed to be only one story high, with thirty classrooms all in a row. Instead, it is thirty stories high, with one classroom on each story.

NARRATOR 3: The builder said he was very sorry.

NARRATOR 1: Our first story is about Joe. One day, Mrs. Jewls kept him in from recess.

MRS. JEWLS: Joe, you are going to have to learn to count.

JOE: But, Mrs. Jewls, I already know how to count. Let me go to recess!

MRS. JEWLS: First count to ten.

NARRATOR 4: Joe counted to ten.

JOE: Six, eight, twelve, one, five, two, seven, eleven, three, ten.

MRS. JEWLS: No, Joe, that is wrong.

JOE: No, it isn't! I counted till I got to ten!

MRS. JEWLS: But you were wrong. I'll prove it to you.

NARRATOR 2: She put down five pencils.

MRS. JEWLS: How many pencils do we have here, Joe?

NARRATOR 3: Joe counted the pencils.

JOE: Four, six, one, nine, five. There are five pencils, Mrs. Jewls.

MRS. JEWLS: That's wrong.

JOE: How many pencils are there?

MRS. JEWLS: Five.

JOE: That's what I said! May I go to recess now?

MRS. JEWLS: No. You got the right answer, but you counted the wrong way. You were just lucky.

NARRATOR 1: She set down eight potatoes.

MRS. JEWLS: How many potatoes, Joe?

NARRATOR 4: Joe counted the potatoes.

JOE: Seven, five, three, one, two, four, six, eight. There are eight potatoes, Mrs. Jewls.

MRS. JEWLS: No, there are eight.

JOE: But that's what I said! May I go to recess now?

MRS. JEWLS: No! You got the right answer, but you counted the wrong way again.

NARRATOR 2: She put down three books.

MRS. JEWLS: Count the books, Joe.

NARRATOR 3: Joe counted the books.

JOE: A thousand, a million, three. Three, Mrs. Jewls.

MRS. JEWLS: (bewildered) Correct.

JOE: May I go to recess now?

MRS. JEWLS: No.

JOE: May I have a potato?

MRS. JEWLS: No! Listen to me. One, two, three, four, five, six, seven, eight, nine, ten. Now you say it.

JOE: One, two, three, four, five, six, seven, eight, nine, ten.

MRS. JEWLS: Very good!

NARRATOR 1: She put down six erasers.

MRS. JEWLS: Now, count the erasers, Joe, just the way I showed you.

NARRATOR 4: Joe counted the erasers.

JOE: One, two, three, four, five, six, seven, eight, nine, ten. There are ten, Mrs. Jewls.

MRS. JEWLS: No!

JOE: Didn't I count right?

MRS. JEWLS: Yes, you counted right, but you got the wrong answer.

JOE: This doesn't make any sense! When I count the wrong way, I get the right answer, and when I count right, I get the wrong answer.

MRS. JEWLS: (in great frustration) Ooh!

NARRATOR 2: Mrs. Jewls hit her head against the wall five times.

MRS. JEWLS: (turning away and butting her head) Uh . . . uh . . . uh . . uh . . . uh . . . (turns back to JOE) How many times did I hit my head against the wall, Joe?

JOE: One, two, three, four, five, six, seven, eight, nine, ten. You hit your head against the wall ten times.

MRS. JEWLS: No!

JOE: Four, six, one, nine, five. You hit your head five times.

NARRATOR 3: Mrs. Jewls shook her head no and said,

MRS. JEWLS: (shaking head) Yes, that is right.

NARRATOR 1: Just then, the bell rang.

JOE: Oh, darn.

NARRATOR 4: . . . said Joe.

JOE: I missed recess!

NARRATOR 3: Our second story is about Bebe.

NARRATOR 1: Bebe was the fastest draw in Mrs. Jewls's class. She could draw a cat in less than fortyfive seconds, a dog in less than thirty, and a flower in less than eight seconds!

NARRATOR 4: But of course, Bebe never drew just one dog, or one cat, or one flower.

NARRATOR 2: Art was from 12:30 to 1:30. Why, in that time, she could draw fifty cats, a hundred flowers, twenty dogs, and several eggs or watermelons!

NARRATOR 3: You see, it took her the same time to draw a watermelon as an egg.

NARRATOR 1: Calvin sat next to Bebe. He didn't think he was very good at art. It took him the whole period just to draw one airplane.

NARRATOR 4: So instead, he just helped Bebe. He was Bebe's assistant.

NARRATOR 2: As soon as Bebe would finish one masterpiece, Calvin would take it from her and set down a clean sheet of paper. Whenever her crayon ran low, Calvin was ready with a new crayon.

NARRATOR 3: That way, Bebe didn't have to waste any time. And in return, Bebe would draw five or six airplanes for Calvin.

NARRATOR 1: It was 12:30, time for art.

NARRATOR 4: Bebe was ready. On her desk was a sheet of yellow construction paper. In her hand was a green crayon.

NARRATOR 2: Calvin was ready. He held a stack of paper and a box of crayons.

CALVIN: Ready, Bebe?

BEBE: Ready, Calvin.

MRS. JEWLS: All right, class.

NARRATOR 3: . . . said Mrs. Jewls.

MRS. JEWLS: Time for art.

NARRATOR 1: She had hardly finished her sentence when Bebe had drawn a picture of a leaf.

NARRATOR 4: Calvin took it from her and put down another piece of paper.

BEBE: Red!

NARRATOR 2: Calvin handed Bebe a red crayon.

BEBE: Blue!

NARRATOR 3: He gave her a blue crayon.

NARRATOR 1: They were quite a pair! Their teamwork was remarkable.

NARRATOR 4: Bebe drew pictures as fast as Calvin could pick up the old paper and set down the new.

NARRATOR 2: A fish.

NARRATOR 3: An apple.

NARRATOR 1: Three cherries—

NARRATOR 4: bing,

NARRATOR 2: bing,

NARRATOR 3: bing.

NARRATOR 1: At 1:30, Mrs. Jewls announced,

MRS. JEWLS: Okay, class, art is over.

NARRATOR 4: Bebe dropped her crayon and fell over on her desk.

NARRATOR 2: Calvin sighed and leaned back in his chair. He could hardly move.

NARRATOR 3: They had broken their old record. Bebe had drawn three hundred and seventyeight pictures! They lay in a pile on Calvin's desk.

NARRATOR 1: Mrs. Jewls walked by.

MRS. JEWLS: Calvin, did you draw all these pictures?

CALVIN: No, Bebe drew them all.

MRS. JEWLS: Well then, what did you draw?

CALVIN: I didn't draw anything.

MRS. JEWLS: Why not? Don't you like art?

CALVIN: I love art. That's why I didn't draw anything.

MRS. JEWLS: I don't understand.

CALVIN: It would have taken me the whole period just to draw one picture. And Bebe would only have been able to draw a hundred pictures. But with the two of us working together, she was able to draw three hundred and seventyeight pictures! That's a lot more art.

NARRATOR 4: Bebe and Calvin shook hands.

MRS. JEWLS: No, no! That isn't how you measure art. It isn't how many pictures you have, but how good the pictures are. Why, a person could spend their whole life drawing just one picture of a cat. In that time, I'm sure Bebe could draw a million cats.

BEBE: Two million.

MRS. JEWLS: But if that one picture is better than each of Bebe's two million, then that person has produced more art than Bebe.

NARRATOR 2: Bebe looked like she was going to cry. She picked up all the pictures from Calvin's desk and threw them in the garbage.

NARRATOR 3: Then she ran from the room, down all the stairs, and out onto the playground.

NARRATOR 1: Louis, the nice yard teacher, spotted her.

LOUIS: Where are you going, Bebe?

BEBE: I'm going home to draw a picture of a cat.

LOUIS: Will you bring it to school and show it to me tomorrow?
BEBE: Tomorrow? By tomorrow I doubt I'll be finished with even one whisker. (rushes off)

NARRATOR 2: Our final story is about Calvin. One day, Mrs. Jewls said,
MRS. JEWLS: Calvin, I want you to take this note to Miss Zarves for me.
CALVIN: Miss Zarves?
MRS. JEWLS: Yes, Miss Zarves. You know where she is, don't you?
CALVIN: Yes. She's on the nineteenth story.
MRS. JEWLS: That's right, Calvin. Take it to her.
NARRATOR 3: Calvin didn't move.
MRS. JEWLS: Well, what are you waiting for?
CALVIN: She's on the nineteenth story.
MRS. JEWLS: Yes, we have already established that fact.
CALVIN: The nineteenth story.
MRS. JEWLS: Yes, Calvin, the nineteenth story. Now take it to her before I lose my patience!
CALVIN: But, Mrs. Jewls—
MRS. JEWLS: NOW, Calvin!
CALVIN: Yes, ma'am!
NARRATOR 1: Calvin walked out of the classroom and stood outside the door.
NARRATOR 4: He didn't know where to go.
NARRATOR 2: As you know, when the builder built Wayside School, he accidentally built it sideways. But he also forgot to build the nineteenth story.
NARRATOR 3: He built the eighteenth and the twentieth, but no nineteenth. He said he was very sorry.
NARRATOR 1: There was also no Miss Zarves.
NARRATOR 4: Miss Zarves taught the class on the nineteenth story. Since there was no nineteenth story, there was no Miss Zarves.
NARRATOR 2: And besides that, as if Calvin didn't have enough problems, there was no note.
NARRATOR 3: Mrs. Jewls had never given Calvin the note.

CALVIN: (sarcastically) Boy, this is just great! I'm supposed to take a note that I don't have, to a teacher who doesn't exist, and who teaches on a story that was never built!

NARRATOR 1: He didn't know what to do.

NARRATOR 4: He walked down to the eighteenth story,

NARRATOR 2: then back up to the twentieth,

NARRATOR 3: then back down to the eighteenth,

NARRATOR 1: and back up again to the twentieth.

NARRATOR 4: There was no nineteenth story.

NARRATOR 2: There had never been a nineteenth story.

NARRATOR 3: There would never BE a nineteenth story.

NARRATOR 1: Calvin walked down to the administration office on the first story. He decided to put the note in Miss Zarves's mailbox.

NARRATOR 4: But there wasn't one of those, either. That didn't bother Calvin too much, though, since he didn't have a note.

NARRATOR 2: He looked out the window and saw Louis, the yard teacher, shooting baskets.

CALVIN: Louis will know what to do.

NARRATOR 3: Calvin went outside.

CALVIN: Hey, Louis!

LOUIS: Hi, Calvin. Do you want to play a game?

CALVIN: I don't have time. I have to deliver a note to Miss Zarves up on the nineteenth story.

LOUIS: Then what are you doing all the way down here?

CALVIN: There is no nineteenth story.

LOUIS: Then where is Miss Zarves?

CALVIN: There is no Miss Zarves.

LOUIS: What are you going to do with the note?

CALVIN: There is no note.

LOUIS: I understand.

CALVIN: That's good, because I sure don't.

LOUIS: It's very simple. You are not supposed to take no notes to no teachers. You already haven't done it!

NARRATOR 1: Calvin still didn't understand.

CALVIN: I'll just have to tell Mrs. Jewls that I couldn't deliver the note.

LOUIS: That's good. The truth is always best. Besides, I don't think I understand what I said, either!

NARRATOR 4: Calvin walked back up the thirty flights of stairs to Mrs. Jewls's class.

MRS. JEWLS: Thank you very much, Calvin.

CALVIN: But I—

MRS. JEWLS: That was a very important note, and I'm glad I was able to count on you.

CALVIN: Yes, but you see—

MRS. JEWLS: The note was very important. I told Miss Zarves not to meet me for lunch.

CALVIN: Don't worry.

NARRATOR 2: . . . said Calvin.

CALVIN: She won't!

NARRATOR 1: So now you know about Wayside School. Some people say these stories are strange and silly.

NARRATOR 4: That is probably true.

NARRATOR 2: But when the children at Wayside School heard stories about us, they thought we were strange and silly.

NARRATOR 3: And that's for sure!

EXERCISE

"Boy, this is just great! I'm supposed to take a note that I don't have, to a teacher who doesn't exist, and who teaches on a story that was never built!"

Aaron Shepard, the children's author has popularised 'Reader's theatre' adapting stories from famous authors such as Louis Sachar. Reader's theatre aims at improving reading skills and fluency of learners. The scripts are meant to be read aloud with vocal expression to make the story intelligible to the audience.

The unreasonable and illogical Sideways Stories for children are silly and funny and the author Louis Sachar himself appears as a character in the stories. The Wayside school was accidentally built sideways thirty stories high instead of thirty rooms in a story and the builder was sorry for it.

A. Expressing Apology

1. You accidentally missed an important meeting. Write an email apologizing to your team.

   Response: "Dear Team, I sincerely apologize for missing today's meeting. It was an oversight on my part, and I understand the inconvenience it caused. I will make sure it doesn't happen again."

2. You unintentionally hurt a friend's feelings with a comment. Write a message apologizing to them.

   Response: "Dear [Friend's Name], I'm really sorry for what I said earlier. I didn't mean to hurt your feelings, and I truly apologize for any pain I caused. Please know that I value our friendship deeply."

3. You were late to an event that someone else organized. Write a note of apology to the organizer.

   Response: "Hi [Organizer's Name], I'm really sorry for being late to your event. I know how much effort you put into organizing it, and I regret not being on time. Please accept my apology."

Verbal Expression Practice

1. You forgot to return a borrowed item on time. Practice how you would verbally apologize to the owner.

   Response: "I'm so sorry I didn't return this sooner. I completely forgot, and I hope it didn't cause any trouble."

2. You missed an appointment with someone. Practice how you would verbally apologize to them.

   Response: "I'm really sorry for missing our appointment. I know your time is valuable, and I apologize for any inconvenience this caused."

B. Expressing Gratitude

1. You received help from a friend during a difficult time. Write a thank-you note expressing your gratitude.

Response: Dear [Friend's Name], I can't thank you enough for being there for me during such a challenging time. Your support meant the world to me, and I'm truly grateful for your kindness and understanding."

2. Your colleague helped you with a project at work. Write a short email thanking them for their assistance.

   Response: "Hi [Colleague's Name], I just wanted to say a big thank you for your help with the project. Your insights and hard work really made a difference, and I appreciate your support!"

3. A stranger found and returned your lost wallet. Write a brief message to express your gratitude.

   Response: "Thank you so much for your honesty and generosity. I'm incredibly grateful for your help!"

Verbal Expression Practice

1. Your friend gave you a thoughtful gift. Practice how you would verbally express your gratitude.

   Response: "Wow, thank you so much for this gift! It's perfect, and it means a lot to me that you thought of me."

2. Your teacher provided you with valuable advice. Practice expressing your gratitude.

   Response: "Thank you so much for your advice. It really helped me see things more clearly, and I'm grateful for your guidance."

Stopping by Woods on a Snowy Evening

Robert Frost

Whose woods these are I think I know.
His house is in the village though;
He will not see me stopping here
To watch his woods fill up with snow.

My little horse must think it queer
To stop without a farmhouse near
Between the woods and frozen lake
The darkest evening of the year.

He gives his harness bells a shake
To ask if there is some mistake.
The only other sound's the sweep
Of easy wind and downy flake.

The woods are lovely, dark and deep,
But I have promises to keep,
And miles to go before I sleep,
And miles to go before I sleep.

Exercise

"But I have promises to keep,
And miles to go before I sleep,"

The poem is one of the greatest poems of the 20th century and it is an all-time favourite. It is about the awareness of the purpose in life and setting goals and accomplishing it. There is a mystery that surrounds the poem regarding the promises that is left unspoken but it makes the speaker in the poem to move on though the woods are lovely, dark, and deep and seem to beckon him to stay on.

A. Describe your village/town/city

About my village/town/city	Few Points on its Significance (Historical/geographical etc.)
Name: Vellore (City)	Sepoy Mutiny – the first instance of a large-scale and violent mutiny by Indian sepoys
District: Vellore	Vellore Fort – built in 1566 under Emperor Sadasiva Raya of the Vijayanagar Empire
State: Tamil Nadu	Leather hub of India with tannery facilities around Vellore and nearby towns such as Ranipet, Ambur and Vaniyambadi

B. Narrate your travel experience following the timeline given below:

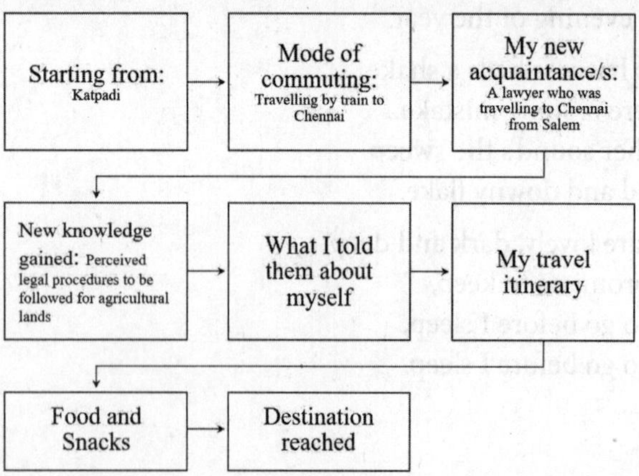

SEMESTER
II

Don't Quit

Edgar Albert Guest

When things go wrong, as they sometimes will,
when the road you're trudging seems all uphill,
when the funds are low and the debts are high,
and you want to smile but you have to sigh,
when care is pressing you down a bit – rest if you must, but don't
you quit.

Life is queer with its twists and turns.
As everyone of us sometimes learns.
And many a fellow turns about when he might have won had he
stuck it out.
Don't give up though the pace seems slow – you may succeed
with another blow.
Often the goal is nearer than it seems to a faint and faltering man;

Often the struggler has given up when he might have captured
the victor's cup;
and he learned too late when the night came down,
how close he was to the golden crown.

Success is failure turned inside out – the silver tint of
the clouds of doubt,

and when you never can tell how close you are,
it may be near when it seems afar;
so stick to the fight when you're hardest hit - it's when
things seem worst, you must not quit.

Exercise

"Life is queer with its twists and turns.
As everyone of us sometimes learns.
And many a fellow turns about when he might
have won had he stuck it out.
Don't give up though the pace seems slow –
you may succeed with another blow."

The poem "Don't Quit" by Edgar A. Guest inspires one to persevere against odds and never be discouraged and to go on with resilience to fight and face the challenges.

A. Strengths, Weaknesses, Opportunities and Challenges (SWOC) Analysis can be made to evaluate and understand one's positive qualities and identify opportunities to improve oneself. Do a SWOC Analysis based on the examples given below to guide you to assess your present situation:

Strengths

1. I am good in Communication skills.
2. I can learn any language quickly
3. I am good at Mathematics.

These are a few examples of Strength. Find out your strength and write down what you are good at.

Weakness

1. I am afraid of talking in front of a group of people.
2. I am weak in English.
3. I find it difficult to talk to new people.

The above are a few examples of Weakness. Find out what is your weakness which you want to remove and list them out.

Opportunity

1. I am a quick learner so I can learn new job techniques quickly.
2. My communication skills are good so I can be a good Soft Skill Trainer.
3. I am good at working with chemicals so I can be a good Lab Assistant.

The above are a few examples of Opportunities. Find out how your strength can create opportunities for you and list them out.

Challenges

1. There are fewer vacancies in the company where I wish to apply for a job.
2. All the seats are reserved in the train and I want to go home.
3. I haven't prepared for my entrance exam. I might fail in it and lose the chance to get admission in Post Graduation.

The above are the examples for challenges. List out the challenges you face in day to day life.

Engine Trouble

R.K. Narayan

There came down to our town some years ago (said the Talkative Man) a showman owning an institution called the Gaiety Land. Overnight our Gymkhana Grounds became resplendent with banners and streamers and coloured lamps. From all over the district crowds poured into the show. Within a week of opening, in gate money alone they collected nearly five hundred rupees a day. Gaiety Land provided us with all sorts of fun and gambling and sideshows. For a couple of annas in each booth we could watch anything from performing parrots to crack motorcyclists looping the loop in the Dome of Death. In addition to this there were lotteries and shooting galleries where for an anna you always stood a chance of winning a hundred rupees. There was a particular corner of the show which was in great favour. Here for a ticket costing eight annas you stood a chance of acquiring a variety of articles—pincushions, sewing machines, cameras or even a road engine. On one evening they drew ticket number 1005, and I happened to own the other half of the ticket. Glancing down the list of articles, they declared that I became the owner of the road engine! Don't ask me how a road engine came to be included among the prizes. It is more than I can tell you. I looked stunned. People gathered round and gazed at me as if I were some curious animal. 'Fancy anyone becoming the owner of a road engine!' some persons muttered, and giggled. It was not the sort of prize one could carry home at short notice. I asked the showman if he would help me to transport it. He merely pointed at a notice which decreed that all winners should remove the prizes immediately on drawing and by their own effort. However, they had to make an exception in my case. They agreed to keep the engine on the Gymkhana Grounds till the end of their season, and then I would have to make my own arrangements to take it out. When I asked the showman if he could find me a driver he just smiled. 'The fellow who brought it here had to be paid a hundred rupees for the job and five rupees a day. I sent him away and made up my mind that if no one was going to draw it, I would just leave it to its fate. I got it down just as a novelty for the show. God! What a bother it has proved!' 'Can't I sell it to some municipality?' I asked innocently. He burst into a laugh. 'As a showman I have enough troubles with municipal people. I would rather keep out of their way . . .' My friends and well-wishers poured in to congratulate me on my latest acquisition. No one knew precisely how much a road engine would fetch; all the same they felt that there was a lot of money in it. 'Even if you sell it as scrap iron you can make a few thousands,' some of my friends declared. Every day I made a trip to the Gymkhana Grounds to have a look at my engine. I grew very fond of it. I loved its shining brass parts. I stood near it and patted it affectionately, hovered about it and returned home every day only at the close of the show. I was a poor man. I thought that, after all, my troubles were coming to an end. How ignorant we are! How little did I guess that my troubles had just begun. When the showman took down his booths and packed up, I received a notice from the municipality to attend to my road engine. When I went there next day it looked forlorn with no one about. The ground was littered with torn streamers and paper decorations. The showman had moved on, leaving the engine where it stood. It was perfectly safe anywhere! I left it alone for a few days, not knowing what to do with it. I received a notice from the municipality ordering that the engine be removed at once from the grounds, as otherwise they would charge rent for the occupation of the Gymkhana Grounds. After deep thought I consented to pay the rent, and I paid ten rupees a month for the next three months. Dear Sirs, I was a poor man. Even the house which I and my wife occupied cost me only four rupees a month. And fancy my paying ten rupees a month for the road engine. It cut into my slender budget, and I had to pledge a jewel or two belonging to my wife! And every day my wife was asking me what I proposed to do with this terrible property of mine and I had no answer to give her. I went up and down the town offering it for sale to all and sundry. Someone suggested that the secretary of the local Cosmopolitan Club might be interested in it. When I approached him he laughed and asked what he could do with a road engine. 'I'll dispose of it at a concession for you. You have a tennis court to be rolled every morning,' I began, and even before I saw him smile I knew it was a stupid thing to say. Next someone suggested, 'See the Municipal Chairman. He may buy it for the municipality.' With great trepidation I went to the municipal office one day. I buttoned up my coat as I entered the chairman's room and mentioned my business. I was prepared to give away the engine at a great concession. I started a great harangue on municipal duties, the regime of this chairman and the importance of owning a road roller—but before I was done with him I knew there was greater chance of my selling it to some child on the roadside for playing with. I was making myself a bankrupt maintaining this engine in the Gymkhana Grounds. I really hoped someday there would come my way a lump sum to make amends for all this deficit and suffering. Fresh complications arose when a cattle show came in the offing. It was to be held on the grounds. I was given twenty-four hours to get the thing out of the grounds. The show was opening in a week and the advance party was arriving and insisted upon having the engine out of the way. I became desperate; there was not a single person for fifty miles around who knew anything about a road engine. I begged every passing bus-driver to help me, but without use. I even approached the station-master to put in a word with the mail engine-driver. But the engine-driver pointed out that he had his own locomotive to mind and couldn't think of jumping off at a wayside station for anybody's sake. Meanwhile, the municipality was pressing me to clear out. I thought it over. I saw the priest of the local temple and managed to gain his sympathy. He offered me the services of his temple elephant. I also engaged fifty coolies to push the engine from behind. You may be sure this drained all my resources. The coolies wanted eight annas per head, and the temple elephant cost me seven rupees a day and I had to give it one feed. My plan was to take the engine out of the Gymkhana and then down the road to a field half a furlong off. The field was owned by a friend. He would not mind if I kept the engine there for a couple of months, when I could go to Madras and find a customer for it. I also took into service one Joseph, a dismissed bus-driver who said that although he knew nothing of road rollers he could nevertheless steer one if it was somehow kept in motion. It was a fine sight: the temple elephant yoked to the engine by means of stout ropes, with fifty determined men pushing it from behind, and my friend Joseph sitting in the driving seat. A huge crowd stood around and watched in great glee. The engine began to move. It seemed to me the greatest moment in my life. When it came out of the Gymkhana and reached the road, it began to behave in a strange manner. Instead of going straight down the road it showed a tendency to wobble and move zigzag. The elephant dragged it one way, Joseph turned the wheel for all he was worth without any idea of where he was going, and fifty men behind it clung to it in every possible manner and pushed it just where they liked. As a result of all this confused dragging, the engine ran straight into the opposite compound wall and reduced a good length of it to powder. At this the crowd let out a joyous yell. The elephant, disliking the behaviour of the crowd, trumpeted loudly, strained and snapped its ropes and kicked down a further length of the wall. The fifty men fled in panic, the crowd created a pandemonium. Someone slapped me in the face—it was the owner of the compound wall. The police came on the scene and marched me off. When I was released from the lockup I found the following consequences awaiting me: (1) several yards of compound wall to be built by me; (2) wages of fifty men who ran away (they would not explain how they were entitled to the wages when they had not done their job); (3) Joseph's fee for steering the engine over the wall; (4) cost of medicine for treating the knee of the temple elephant, which had received some injuries while kicking down the wall (here again the temple authorities would not listen when I pointed out that I didn't engage an elephant to break a wall); (5) last, but not least, the demand to move the engine out of its present station. Sirs, I was a poor man. I really could not find any means of paying these bills. When I went home my wife asked, 'What is this I hear about you everywhere?' I took the opportunity to explain my difficulties. She took it as a hint that I was again asking for her jewels, and she lost her temper and cried that she would write to her father to come and take her away. I was at my wits' end. People smiled at me when they met me in the streets. I was seriously wondering why I should not run away to my village. I decided to encourage my wife to write to her father and arrange for her exit. Not a soul was going to know what my plans were. I was going to put off my creditors and disappear one fine night. At this point came unexpected relief in the shape of a Swamiji. One fine evening under the distinguished patronage of our Municipal Chairman a show was held in our small town hall. It was a free performance and the hall was packed with people. I sat in the gallery. Spellbound we witnessed the Swamiji's yogic feats. He bit off glass tumblers and ate them with contentment; he lay on spike boards; gargled and drank all kinds of acids; licked white-hot iron rods; chewed and swallowed sharp nails; stopped his heartbeat and buried himself underground. We sat there and watched him in stupefaction. At the end of it all he got up and delivered a speech in which he declared that he was carrying on his master's message to the people in this manner. His performance was the more remarkable because he had nothing to gain by all this extraordinary meal except the satisfaction of serving humanity, and now he said he was coming to the very masterpiece and the last act. He looked at the Municipal Chairman and asked, 'Have you a road engine? I would like to have it driven over my chest.' The chairman looked abashed and felt ashamed to acknowledge that he had none. The Swamiji insisted, 'I must have a road engine.' The Municipal Chairman tried to put him off by saying, 'There is no driver.' The Swamiji replied, 'Don't worry about it. My assistant has been trained to handle any kind of road engine. ' At this point I stood up in the gallery and shouted, 'Don't ask him for an engine. Ask me.' In a moment I was on the stage and became as important a person as the fire-eater himself. I was pleased with the recognition I now received from all quarters. The Municipal Chairman went into the background. In return for lending him the engine he would drive it where I wanted. Though I felt inclined to ask for a money contribution I knew it would be useless to expect it from one who was doing missionary work. Soon the whole gathering was at the compound wall opposite the Gymkhana. Swamiji's assistant was an expert in handling engines. In a short while my engine stood steaming up proudly. It was a gratifying sight. The Swamiji called for two pillows, placed one near his head and the other at his feet. He gave detailed instructions as to how the engine should be run over him. He made a chalk mark on his chest and said, 'It must go exactly on this; not an inch this way or that.' The engine hissed and waited. The crowd watching the show became suddenly unhappy and morose. This seemed to be a terrible thing to be doing. The Swamiji lay down on the pillows and said, 'When I say Om, drive it on.' He closed his eyes. The crowd watched tensely. I looked at the whole show in absolute rapture—after all, the road engine was going to get on the move. At this point a police inspector came into the crowd with a brown envelope in his hand. He held up his hand, beckoned to the Swamiji's assistant and said, 'I am sorry, I have to tell you that you can't go on with this. The magistrate has issued an order prohibiting the engine from running over him.' The Swamiji picked himself up. There was a lot of commotion. The Swamiji became indignant. 'I have done it in hundreds of places already and nobody questioned me about it. Nobody can stop me from doing what I like—it's my master's order to demonstrate the power of the Yoga to the people of this country, and who can question me?' 'A magistrate can,' said the police inspector, and held up the order. 'What business is it of yours or his to interfere in this manner?' 'I don't know all that; this is his order. He permits you to do everything except swallow potassium cyanide and run this engine over your chest. You are free to do whatever you like outside our jurisdiction.' 'I am leaving this cursed place this very minute,' the Swamiji said in great rage, and started to go, followed by his assistant. I gripped his assistant's arm and said,

'You have steamed it up. Why not take it over to that field and then go.' He glared at me, shook off my hand and muttered, 'With my guru so unhappy, how dare you ask me to drive?' He went away. I muttered, 'You can't drive it except over his chest, I suppose?' I made preparations to leave the town in a couple of days, leaving the engine to its fate, with all its commitments. However, nature came to my rescue in an unexpected manner. You may have heard of the earthquake of that year which destroyed whole towns in North India. There was a reverberation of it in our town, too. We were thrown out of our beds that night, and doors and windows rattled. Next morning I went over to take a last look at my engine before leaving the town. I could hardly believe my eyes. The engine was not there. I looked about and raised a hue and cry. Search parties went round. The engine was found in a disused well nearby, with its back up. I prayed to heaven to save me from fresh complications. But the owner of the house, when he came round and saw what had happened, laughed heartily and beamed at me. 'You have done me a service. It was the dirtiest water on earth in that well and the municipality was sending notice to close it, week after week. I was dreading the cost of closing, but your engine fits it like a cork. Just leave it there.' 'But, but . . .' 'There are no buts. I will withdraw all complaints and charges against you, and build that broken wall myself, but only leave the thing there.' 'That's hardly enough.' I mentioned a few other expenses that this engine had brought on me. He agreed to pay for all that. When I again passed that way some months later I peeped over the wall. I found the mouth of the well neatly cemented up. I heaved a sigh of great relief.

Exercise

"People gathered round and gazed at me as if I were some curious animal. 'Fancy anyone becoming the owner of a road engine!'"

The ironic story is about a person called the talkative man winning an unusual prize, a road engine, and the ordeals he had to face on account of winning it. The prize won in the lottery brings more trouble than prosperity and the hilarious story ends up bringing relief to the winner when an earthquake solves his problem of having to find a place to shift it when it becomes the cover for an unused well.

A. Self esteem

"Mirror, Mirror on the wall, I'll always get up even if I fall. Whether I run, walk, or have to crawl, I'll set my goals and achieve them all. I value myself after all"

Replace your negative thoughts with positive affirmations and add your own to the list. Stand before the mirror, look at your eyes, and affirm these statements.

Negative Thought	Positive Affirmation
I'm unloved	I am loved
I'm ugly	My appearance does not define me

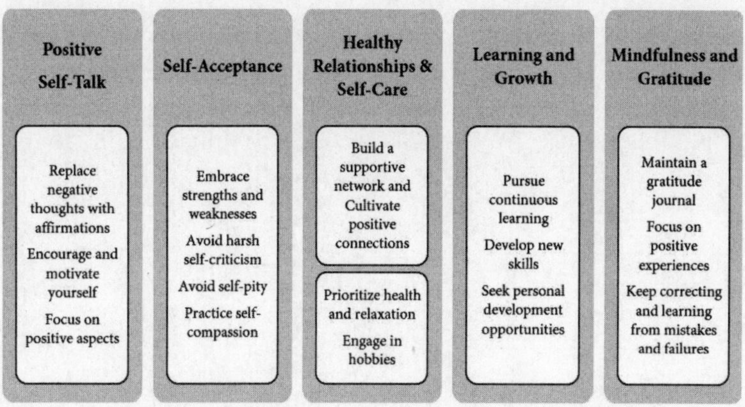

B. Find the hidden words:

A	K	P	A	N	D	E	M	O	N	I	U	M
G	J	G	Y	M	K	H	A	N	A	M	L	U
J	H	H	T	R	E	N	N	A	B	N	K	N
T	G	T	G	F	D	K	L	D	E	B	J	I
E	F	Y	T	N	E	M	T	I	M	M	O	C
K	D	R	N	V	N	K	R	C	M	C	H	I
C	S	E	E	L	G	J	O	V	N	V	G	P
I	A	W	B	D	I	H	U	S	B	C	F	A
T	P	U	R	K	N	A	B	E	V	Z	D	L
G	J	Q	C	W	E	F	L	F	C	A	S	I
R	G	W	X	O	R	D	E	T	X	S	A	T
E	T	E	Z	P	U	Y	T	R	E	W	Q	Y

Wings of Fire

A.P.J. Abdul Kalam

I was born into a middle-class Tamil family in the island town of Rameswaram in the erstwhile Madras state. My father, Jainulabdeen, had neither much formal education nor much wealth; despite these disadvantages, he possessed great innate wisdom and a true generosity of spirit. He had an ideal helpmate in my mother, Ashiamma. I do not recall the exact number of people she fed every day, but I am quite certain that far more outsiders ate with us than all the members of our own family put together. My parents were widely regarded as an ideal couple. My mother's lineage was the more distinguished, one of her forebears having been bestowed the title of 'Bahadur' by the British. I was one of many children—a short boy with rather undistinguished looks, born to tall and handsome parents. We lived in our ancestral house, which was built in the middle of the 19th century. It was a fairly large pucca house, made of limestone and brick, on the Mosque Street in Rameswaram. My austere father used to avoid all inessential comforts and luxuries. However, all necessities were provided for, in terms of food, medicine or clothes. In fact, I would say mine was a very secure childhood, both materially and emotionally. I normally ate with my mother, sitting on the floor of the kitchen. She would place a banana leaf before me, on which she then ladled rice and aromatic sambhar, a variety of sharp, home-made pickles and a dollop of fresh coconut chutney. The famous Shiva temple, which made Rameswaram so sacred to pilgrims, was about a ten-minute walk from our house. Our locality was predominantly Muslim, but there were quite a few Hindu families too, living amicably with their Muslim neighbours. There was a very old mosque in our locality where my father would take me for evening prayers. I had not the faintest idea of the meaning of the Arabic prayers chanted, but I was totally convinced that they reached God. When my father came out of the mosque after the prayers, people of different religions would be sitting outside, waiting for him. Many of them offered bowls of water to my father who would dip his fingertips in them and say a prayer. This water was then carried home for invalids. I also remember people visiting our home to offer thanks after being cured. My father always smiled and asked them to thank Allah, the benevolent and merciful. The high priest of Rameswaram temple, Pakshi Lakshmana Sastry, was a very close friend of my father's. One of the most vivid memories of my early childhood is of the two men, each in his traditional attire, discussing spiritual matters. When I was old enough to ask questions, I asked my father about the relevance of prayer. My father told me there was nothing mysterious about prayer. Rather, prayer made possible a communion of the spirit between people. "When you pray," he said, "you transcend your body and become a part of the cosmos, which knows no division of wealth, age, caste, or creed." My father could convey complex spiritual concepts in very simple, down-to-earth Tamil. He once told me, "In his own time, in his own place, in what he really is, and in the stage he has reached—good or bad—every human being is a specific element within the whole of the manifest divine Being. So why be afraid of difficulties, sufferings and problems? When troubles come, try to understand the relevance of your sufferings. Adversity always presents opportunities for introspection." "Why don't you say this to the people who come to you for help and advice?" I asked my father. He put his hands on my shoulders and looked straight into my eyes. For quite some time he said nothing, as if he was judging my capacity to comprehend his words. Then he answered in a low, deep voice. His answer filled me with a strange energy and enthusiasm: Whenever human beings find themselves alone, as a natural reaction, they start looking for company. Whenever they are in trouble, they look for someone to help them. Whenever they reach an impasse, they look to someone to show them the way out. Every recurrent anguish, longing, and desire finds its own special helper. For the people who come to me in distress, I am but a go-between in their effort to propitiate demonic forces with prayers and offerings. This is not a correct approach at all and should never be followed. One must understand the difference between a fear-ridden vision of destiny and the vision that enables us to seek the enemy of fulfilment within ourselves. I remember my father starting his day at 4 a.m. by reading the namaz before dawn. After the namaz, he used to walk down to a small coconut grove we owned, about 4 miles from our home. He would return, with about a dozen coconuts tied together thrown over his shoulder, and only then would he have his breakfast. This remained his routine even when he was in his late sixties. I have throughout my life tried to emulate my father in my own world of science and technology. I have endeavoured to understand the fundamental truths revealed to me by my father, and feel convinced that there exists a divine power that can lift one up from confusion, misery, melancholy and failure, and guide one to one's true place. And once an individual severs his emotional and physical bondage, he is on the road to freedom, happiness and peace of mind. I was about six years old when my father embarked on the project of building a wooden sailboat to take pilgrims from Rameswaram to Dhanuskodi, (also called Sethukkarai), and back. He worked at building the boat on the seashore, with the help of a relative, Ahmed Jallaluddin, who later married my sister, Zohara. I watched the boat take shape. The wooden hull and bulkheads were seasoned with the heat from wood fires. My father was doing good business with the boat when, one day, a cyclone bringing winds of over 100 miles per hour carried away our boat, along with some of the landmass of Sethukkarai. The Pamban Bridge collapsed with a train full of passengers on it. Until then, I had only seen the beauty of the sea, now its uncontrollable energy came as a revelation to me. By the time the boat met its untimely end, Ahmed Jallaluddin had become a close friend of mine, despite the difference in our ages. He was about 15 years older than I and used to call me Azad. We used to go for long walks together every evening. As we started from Mosque Street and made our way towards the sandy shores of the island, Jallaluddin and I talked mainly of spiritual matters. The atmosphere of Rameswaram, with its flocking pilgrims, was conducive to such discussion. Our first halt would be at the imposing temple of Lord Shiva. Circling around the temple with the same reverence as any pilgrim from a distant part of the country, we felt a flow of energy pass through us. Jallaluddin would talk about God as if he had a working partnership with Him. He would present all his doubts to God as if He were standing nearby to dispose of them. I would stare at Jallaluddin and then look towards the large groups of pilgrims around the temple, taking holy dips in the sea, performing rituals and reciting prayers with a sense of respect towards the same Unknown, whom we treat as the formless Almighty. I never doubted that the prayers in the temple reached the same destination as the ones offered in our mosque. I only wondered whether Jallaluddin had any other special connection to God. Jallaluddin's schooling had been limited, principally because of his family's straitened circumstances. This may have been the reason why he always encouraged me to excel in my studies and enjoyed my success vicariously. Never did I find the slightest trace of resentment in Jallaluddin for his deprivation. Rather, he was always full of gratitude for whatever life had chosen to give him. Incidentally, at the time I speak of, he was the only person on the entire island who could write English. He wrote letters for almost anybody in need, be they letters of application or otherwise. Nobody of my acquaintance, either in my family or in the neighbourhood even had Jallaluddin's level of education or any links of consequence with the outside world. Jallaluddin always spoke to me about educated people, of scientific discoveries, of contemporary literature, and of the achievements of medical science. It was he who made me aware of a "brave, new world" beyond our narrow confines. In the humble environs of my boyhood, books were a scarce commodity. By local standards, however, the personal library of STR Manickam, a former 'revolutionary' or militant nationalist, was sizeable. He encouraged me to read all I could and I often visited his home to borrow books. Another person who greatly influenced my boyhood was my first cousin, Samsuddin. He was the sole distributor for newspapers in Rameswaram. The newspapers would arrive at Rameswaram station by the morning train from Pamban. Samsuddin's newspaper agency was a one-man organization catering to the reading demands of the 1,000-strong literate population of Rameswaram town. These newspapers were mainly bought to keep abreast of current developments in the National Independence Movement, for astrological reference or to check the bullion rates prevailing in Madras. A few readers with a more cosmopolitan outlook would discuss Hitler, Mahatma Gandhi and Jinnah; almost all would finally flow into the mighty political current of Periyar EV Ramaswamy's movement against high caste Hindus. Dinamani was the most sought after newspaper. Since reading the printed matter was beyond my capability, I had to satisfy myself with glancing at the pictures in the newspaper before Samsuddin delivered them to his customers. The Second World War broke out in 1939, when I was eight years old. For reasons I have never been able to understand, a sudden demand for tamarind seeds erupted in the market. I used to collect the seeds and sell them to a provision shop on Mosque Street. A day's collection would fetch me the princely sum of one anna. Jallaluddin would tell me stories about the war which I would later attempt to trace in the headlines in Dinamani. Our area, being isolated, was completely unaffected by the war. But soon India was forced to join the Allied Forces and something like a state of emergency was declared. The first casualty came in the form of the suspension of the train halt at Rameswaram station. The newspapers now had to be bundled and thrown out from the moving train on the Rameswaram Road between Rameswaram and Dhanuskodi. That forced Samsuddin to look for a helping hand to catch the bundles and, as if naturally, I filled the slot. Samsuddin helped me earn my first wages. Half a century later, I can still feel the surge of pride in earning my own money for the first time. Every child is born, with some inherited characteristics, into a specific socio-economic and emotional environment, and trained in certain ways by figures of authority. I inherited honesty and self-discipline from my father; from my mother, I inherited faith in goodness and deep kindness and so did my three brothers and sister. But it was the time I spent with Jallaluddin and Samsuddin that perhaps contributed most to the uniqueness of my childhood and made all the difference in my later life. The unschooled wisdom of Jallaluddin and Samsuddin was so intuitive and responsive to non-verbal messages, that I can unhesitatingly attribute my subsequently manifested creativity to their company in my childhood. I had three close friends in my childhood—Ramanadha Sastry, Aravindan, and Sivaprakasan. All these boys were from orthodox Hindu Brahmin families. As children, none of us ever felt any difference amongst ourselves because of our religious differences and upbringing. In fact, Ramanadha Sastry was the son of Pakshi Lakshmana Sastry, the high priest of the Rameswaram temple. Later, he took over the priesthood of the Rameswaram temple from his father; Aravindan went into the business of arranging transport for visiting pilgrims; and Sivaprakasan became a catering contractor for the Southern Railways. During the annual Shri Sita Rama Kalyanam ceremony, our family used to arrange boats with a special platform for carrying idols of the Lord from the temple to the marriage site, situated in the middle of the pond called Rama Tirtha which was near our house. Events from the Ramayana and from the life of the Prophet were the bedtime stories my mother and grandmother would tell the children in our family. One day when I was in the fifth standard at the Rameswaram Elementary School, a new teacher came to our class. I used to wear a cap which marked me as a Muslim, and I always sat in the front row next to Ramanadha Sastry, who wore a sacred thread. The new teacher could not stomach a Hindu priest's son sitting with a Muslim boy. In accordance with our social ranking as the new teacher saw it, I was asked to go and sit on the back bench. I felt very sad, and so did Ramanadha Sastry. He looked utterly downcast as I shifted to my seat in the last row. The image of him weeping when I shifted to the last row left a lasting impression on me. After school, we went home and told our respective parents about the incident. Lakshmana Sastry summoned the teacher, and in our presence, told the teacher that he should not spread the poison of social inequality and communal intolerance in the minds of innocent children. He bluntly asked the teacher to either apologize or quit the school and the island. Not only did the teacher regret his behaviour, but the strong sense of conviction Lakshmana Sastry conveyed ultimately reformed this young teacher. On the whole, the small society of Rameswaram was highly stratified and very rigid in terms of the segregation of different social groups. However, my science teacher Sivasubramania Iyer, though an orthodox Brahmin with a very conservative wife, was something of a rebel. He did his best to break social barriers so that people from varying backgrounds could mingle easily. He used to spend hours with me and would say, "Kalam, I want you to develop so that you are on par with the highly educated people of the big cities." One day, he invited me to his home for a meal. His wife was horrified at the idea of a Muslim boy being invited to dine in her ritually pure kitchen. She refused to serve me in her kitchen. Sivasubramania Iyer was not perturbed, nor did he get angry with his wife, but instead, served me with his own hands and sat down beside me to eat his meal. His wife watched us from behind the kitchen door. I wondered whether she had observed any difference in the way I ate rice, drank water or cleaned the floor after the meal. When I was leaving his house, Sivasubramania Iyer invited me to join him for dinner again the next weekend. Observing my hesitation, he told me not to get upset, saying, "Once you decide to change the system, such problems have to be confronted." When I visited his house the next week, Sivasubramania Iyer's wife took me inside her kitchen and served me food with her own hands. Then the Second World War was over and India's freedom was imminent. "Indians will build their own India," declared Gandhiji. The whole country was filled with an unprecedented optimism. I asked my father's permission to leave Rameswaram and study at the district headquarters in Ramanathapuram. He told me as if thinking aloud, "Abul! I know you have to go away to grow. Does the seagull not fly across the Sun, alone and without a nest? You must forego your longing for the land of your memories to move into the dwelling place of your greater desires; our love will not bind you nor will our needs hold you." He quoted Khalil Gibran to my hesitant mother, "Your children are not your children. They are the sons and daughters of Life's longing for itself. They come through you but not from you. You may give them your love but not your thoughts. For they have their own thoughts." He took me and my three brothers to the mosque and recited the prayer Al Fatiha from the Holy Qur'an. As he put me on the train at Rameswaram station he said, "This island may be housing your body but not your soul. Your soul dwells in the house of tomorrow which none of us at Rameswaram can visit, not even in our dreams. May God bless you, my child!" Samsuddin and Ahmed Jallaluddin travelled with me to Ramanathapuram to enrol me in Schwartz High School, and to arrange for my boarding there. Somehow, I did not take to the new setting. The town of Ramanathapuram was a thriving, factious town of some fifty thousand people, but the coherence and harmony of Rameswaram was absent. I missed my home and grabbed every opportunity to visit Rameswaram. The pull of educational opportunities at Ramanathapuram was not strong enough to nullify the attraction of poli, a South Indian sweet my mother made. In fact, she used to prepare twelve distinctly different varieties of it, bringing out the flavour of every single ingredient used in the best possible combinations. Despite my homesickness, I was determined to come to terms with the new environment because I knew my father had invested great hopes in my success. My father visualized me as a Collector in the making and I thought it my duty to realise my father's dream, although I desperately missed the familiarity, security and comforts of Rameswaram. Jallaluddin used to speak to me about the power of positive thinking and I often recalled his words when I felt homesick or dejected. I tried hard to do as he said, which was to strive to control my thoughts and my mind and, through these, to influence my destiny. Ironically, that destiny did not lead me back to Rameswaram, but rather, swept me farther away from the home of my childhood.

Exercise

"Every child is born, with some inherited characteristics, into a specific socio-economic and emotional environment, and trained in certain ways by figures of authority."

The autobiography of the eleventh former president of India fondly known as 'Missile Man' is a narrative recounted by Dr.Kalam to Arun Tiwari who put in his best efforts to make the readers connect with a great soul who ignited young minds through his farsighted vision for the nation.

A. Identify the Characters in the Wings of Fire and sketch a family tree.

B. Write a reflective journal entry exploring how Kalam's early life experiences shaped his leadership style from Dr. Kalam's perspective or from your experience inspired by his life.

Reflective Journal Writing

A reflective diary is a personal record of ideas, thoughts, experiences, reflections, and insights that help identify significant learning moments and sources of inspiration.

Journaling helps to	*To start reflective journaling*
• Process and organize thoughts • Develop critical thinking and awareness • Clarify values and goals	• Set aside dedicated time • Write freely without editing or judgments • Explore thoughts, feelings and connections • Reflect, learn, and grow

Reflective Journal Process

Example:

- **What?** As I read about Kalam's childhood, I was impressed by the influence of family and community on his values and goals. His parents' emphasis on education and self-discipline resonates with me, as my own parents instilled similar values. I'm inspired by Kalam's curiosity and determination to study despite obstacles, and I can relate it to my own learning experience. The phrase "The best way to predict your future is to create it" is meaningful to me as I consider my future plans and goals, realizing that I have the power to shape my own destiny.
- **So What?** His family and inspirational people shaped his childhood. It sets the foundation for understanding Kalam's values, beliefs, and motivations, which drove him to become the person he was. It showcased the importance of family, community and education in shaping a person and one's future.

Questions for Reflection

- What values or lessons from Kalam's childhood can I apply to my own life?
- How can I cultivate a similar sense of curiosity and determination in my own learning journey?
- What steps can I take to create the future I want rather than just waiting for it to happen?

What's Next?

- I need to prioritize self-discipline and time management to achieve my goals.
- I should seek out mentors or role models who can guide me in my journey.
- I have the power to create my own future, and I should take ownership of that.

With the Photographer

Stephen Leacock

"I want my photograph taken," I said. The photographer looked at me without enthusiasm. He was a drooping man in a gray suit, with the dim eye of a natural scientist. But there is no need to describe him. Everybody knows what a photographer is like.

"Sit there," he said, "and wait."

I waited an hour. I read the Ladies Companion for 1912, the Girls Magazine for 1902 and the Infants Journal for 1888. I began to see that I had done an unwarrantable thing in breaking in on the privacy of this man's scientific pursuits with a face like mine.

After an hour the photographer opened the inner door.

"Come in," he said severely.

I went into the studio.

"Sit down," said the photographer.

I sat down in a beam of sunlight filtered through a sheet of factory cotton hung against a frosted skylight.

The photographer rolled a machine into the middle of the room and crawled into it from behind.

He was only in it a second, – just time enough for one look at me, – and then he was out again, tearing at the cotton sheet and the window panes with a hooked stick, apparently frantic for light and air.

Then he crawled back into the machine again and drew a little black cloth over himself. This time he was very quiet in there. I knew that he was praying and I kept still.

When the photographer came out at last, he looked very grave and shook his head.

"The face is quite wrong," he said.

"I know," I answered quietly; "I have always known it." He sighed. "I think," he said, "the face would be better three-quarters full."

"I'm sure it would," I said enthusiastically, for I was glad to find that the man had such a human side to him. "So would yours. In fact," I continued, "how many faces one sees that are apparently hard, narrow, limited, but the minute you get them three-quarters full they get wide, large, almost boundless in ..."

But the photographer had ceased to listen. He came over and took my head in his hands and twisted it sideways. I thought he meant to kiss me, and I closed my eyes.

But I was wrong.

He twisted my face as far as it would go and then stood looking at it.

He sighed again.

"I don't like the head," he said.

Then he went back to the machine and took another look.

"Open the mouth a little," he said.

I started to do so.

"Close it," he added quickly.

Then he looked again.

"The ears are bad," he said; "droop them a little more. Thank you. Now the eyes. Roll them in under the lids. Put the hands on the knees, please, and turn the face just a little upward. Yes, that's better. Now just expand the lungs! So! And hump the neck – that's it – and just contract the waist – ha! – and twist the hip up toward the elbow – now! I still don't quite like the face, it's just a trifle too full, but ..."

I swung myself round on the stool.

"Stop," I said with emotion but, I think, with dignity. "This face is my face. It is not yours, it is mine. I've lived with it for forty years and I know its faults. I know it's out of drawing. I know it wasn't made for me, but it's my face, the only one I have ..." I was conscious of a break in my voice but I went on ... "such as it is, I've learned to love it. And this is my mouth, not yours. These ears are mine, and if your machine is too narrow ..." Here I started to rise from the seat.

Snick!

The photographer had pulled a string. The photograph taken. I could see the machine still staggering from the shock.

"I think," said the photographer, pursing his lips in a pleased smile, "that I caught the features just in a moment of animation."

"So!" I said bitingly – "features, eh? You didn't think I could animate them, I suppose? But let me see the picture."

"Oh, there's nothing to see yet," he said, "I have to develop the negative first. Come back on Saturday and I'll let you see a proof of it."

On Saturday I went back.

The photographer beckoned me in. I thought he seemed quieter and graver than before. I think, too, there was a certain pride in his manner.

He unfolded the proof of a large photograph, and we both looked at it in silence.

"Is it me?" I asked.

"Yes," he said quietly, "it is you," and we went on looking at it.

"The eyes," I said hesitatingly, "don't look very much like mine."

"Oh, no," he answered, "I've retouched them. They come out splendidly, don't they?"

"Fine," I said, "but surely my eyebrows are not like that?"

"No," said the photographer, with a momentary glance at my face, "the eyebrows are removed. We have a process now – the Delphide – for putting in new ones. You'll notice here where we've applied it to carry the hair away from the brow. I don't like the hair low on the skull."

"Oh, you don't, don't you?" I said.

"No," he went on, "I don't care for it. I like to get the hair clear back to the superficies and make out a new brow line."

"What about the mouth?" I said with a bitterness that was lost on the photographer; "is that mine?"

"It's adjusted a little," he said, "yours is too low. I found I couldn't use it."

"The ears, though," I said, "strike me as a good likeness; they're just like mine. Is it me?"

"Yes," said the photographer thoughtfully, "that's so; but I can fix that all right in the print. We have a process now – the Sulphide – for removing the ears entirely. I'll see if ..."

"Listen!" I interrupted, drawing myself up and animating my features to their full extent and speaking with a withering scorn that should have blasted the man on the spot. "Listen! I came here for a photograph – a picture – something which (mad though it seems) would have looked like me. I wanted something that would depict my face as Heaven gave it to me, humble though the gift may have been. I wanted something that my friends might keep after my death, to reconcile them to my loss. It seems that I was mistaken. What I wanted is no longer done. Go on, then, with your brutal work. Take your negative, or whatever it is you call it, – dip it in sulphide, bromide, oxide, cowhide, – anything you like, – remove the eyes, correct the mouth, adjust the face, restore the lips, reanimate the necktie and reconstruct the waistcoat. Coat it with an inch of gloss, shade it, emboss it, gild it, till even you acknowledge that it is finished. Then when you have done all that – keep it for yourself and your friends. They may value it. To me it is but a worthless bauble."

I broke into tears and left.

Exercise

"Stop," I said with emotion but, I think, with dignity.
"This face is my face. It is not yours, it is mine.
I've lived with it for forty years and I know its faults."

The narrator visits a photographer's studio to have his portrait taken. The photographer criticizes the narrator's face, eyes, ears, mouth, and even posture for photographic perfection.

A. Debate Writing – For/Against

"Photographs should capture the truth, not perfection".

(i) In favour of the statement

(ii) Against the statement.

B. Vocabulary in Context

Find the meaning of the words/phrases from the story given below and use each of them in a sentence of your own:

Words/Phrases	Meaning	Your sentence
Drooping		
Retouched		
Snick		
Withering scorn		
Bauble		

C. Dialogue Writing

Imagine the narrator returns to the studio a week later after the photo was taken and write a dialogue between the narrator and the photographer arguing about the final photograph.

The Bangle Sellers

Sarojini Naidu

Bangle sellers are we who bear
Our shining loads to the temple fair...
Who will buy these delicate, bright
Rainbow-tinted circles of light?
Lustrous tokens of radiant lives,
For happy daughters and happy wives.

Some are meet for a maiden's wrist,
Silver and blue as the mountain mist,
Some are flushed like the buds that dream
On the tranquil brow of a woodland stream,
Some are aglow with the bloom that cleaves
To the limpid glory of new born leaves.

Some are like fields of sunlit corn,
Meet for a bride on her bridal morn,
Some, like the flame of her marriage fire,
Or, rich with the hue of her heart's desire,
Tinkling, luminous, tender, and clear,
Like her bridal laughter and bridal tear.

Some are purple and gold flecked grey
For she who has journeyed through life midway,
Whose hands have cherished, whose love has blest,
And cradled fair sons on her faithful breast,
And serves her household in fruitful pride,
And worships the gods at her husband's side.

Celebration of Womanhood

Sarojini Naidu, known as "The Nightingale of India", celebrates womanhood in this poem. The poem illustrates the journey and the roles a woman embodies throughout her life, from daughter to wife to mother, by drawing parallels with vibrant bangles.

The activities given below outline the various phases of a woman's life and her roles. According to your observation, which are the responsibilities a woman is expected to carry out at each phase. Make an attempt to portray the emotional state of a woman during each stage.

1. **Infancy**
    - Growing – Physical growth, motor skills, attachment
    - Innocent
    - Lovable
    - Happy
    - peaceful
2. **Childhood**
    - Learning – morality, cognitive, social, emotional development
    - ____________________
    - ____________________
    - ____________________
3. **Teenage**
    - Exploring – self, beliefs, physical changes, independence
    - ____________________
    - ____________________
    - ____________________
4. **Adolescence**
    - Establishing – identity, self-esteem, values

- ______________________
- ______________________
- ______________________

5. **Middle Age**
   - Progressing – career, family, life choices
   - ______________________
   - ______________________
   - ______________________

6. **Old Age**
   - Adjusting – changes, health challenges
   - ______________________
   - ______________________
   - ______________________

List the responsibilities and nature of a woman expected in the following roles:

Daughter	Friend	Wife	Mother

How do you want to exercise your role in the

Family | College | Society | Nation

Still Here

Langston Hughes

I been scared and battered.
My hopes the wind done scattered.
Snow has friz me,
Sun has baked me,

Looks like between 'em they done
Tried to make me

Stop laughin', stop lovin', stop livin'—
But I don't care!
I'm still here!

EXERCISE

"Stop laughin', stop lovin', stop livin'—
But I don't care!
I'm still here!"

The poem ends on an assertive note that celebrates the endurance of the African Americans against all oppression to stand tall and prove the indomitable human spirit and ability to dare injustice and discrimination. The poem provides an opportunity to compare people and situations and identify the similarities and through contrast to know the differences.

A. Writing on Comparison and contrast of people or situations

Writing Exercise: Comparison and Contrast of People or Situations

Comparing Two Friends

- **Title:** A Tale of Two Friends: Sarah and Emily
- Introduction:
  - Introduce both friends briefly.
  - Mention that while they share common interests, their personalities, and approaches to life differ significantly.
- Paragraph 1: Similarities
  - Interests: Both Sarah and Emily enjoy reading, hiking, and cooking.
  - Values: They both value honesty, loyalty, and kindness in friendships.
- Paragraph 2: Differences in Personality
  - Sarah: Extrovert, loves social gatherings, thrives in busy environments.
  - Emily: Introvert, prefers quiet evenings at home, enjoys solitude.
- Paragraph 3: Differences in Approach to Challenges
  - Sarah: Faces challenges head-on, often acts impulsively, relies on gut instincts.
  - Emily: Takes a more cautious approach, analyzes situations before acting, relies on planning.
- Conclusion:
  - Summarize how their differences complement each other and strengthen their friendship.
  - Reflect on how their friendship shows that differences can enhance relationships.

B. Comparing Two Life Situations

- **Title:** City Life vs. Country Life

- Introduction:
  - Briefly introduce the two types of living environments.
  - Mention that both have their unique advantages and challenges.
- Paragraph 1: Similarities
  - Access to Amenities: Both city and country life offer access to basic necessities like grocery stores, schools, and healthcare.
  - Community: In both settings, people can build strong community ties and friendships.
- Paragraph 2: Differences in Pace of Life
  - City Life: Fast-paced, busy, and often stressful; offers more job opportunities and cultural events.
  - Country Life: Slower, more relaxed, offers a connection to nature, and has less pollution.
- Paragraph 3: Differences in Living Space
  - City Life: Often involves living in apartments or smaller homes, with limited outdoor space.
  - Country Life: Typically offers larger homes and more outdoor space, ideal for gardening and outdoor activities.
- Conclusion:
  - Summarize how both city and country life have their pros and cons.
  - Reflect on how personal preferences and lifestyle choices play a significant role in determining which environment might be more suitable for an individual.

Rip Van Winkle

Washington Irving

In a village in the Catskill Mountains, there lived a simple, good-natured fellow by the name of Rip Van Winkle. He was a kind neighbor, and the children would shout with joy whenever he approached. The great fault in Rip's nature, though, was his aversion to profitable labor. He did not lack diligence or perseverance: he would sit on a wet rock holding a long and heavy rod and fish all day even if he never got a single nibble. He trudged for hours through woods and swamps to shoot a few squirrels or wild pigeons. He would never refuse to assist a neighbor even in the roughest toil. In fact, Rip was ready to attend to anybody's business but his own. But as to keeping his own farm in order, he found it impossible, and his children were as ragged as if they belonged to nobody. Rip was one of those happy fools who take the world easy, eat white bread or brown, whichever can be got with least thought or trouble, and would rather starve on a penny than work for a pound. If left to himself, he would have whistled his life away in perfect contentment, but his wife was continually dinning in his ears about his idleness, his carelessness, and the ruin he was bringing on his family. Rip would shrug his shoulders, shake his head, cast up his eyes, but say nothing. This always provoked a fresh volley from his wife, so that he left the house to go outside—

the only side which belongs to a henpecked husband. Rip used to console himself, when driven from home, with the company of a group of sages and fellow idlers who convened on a bench in front of an inn. Sitting beneath a portrait of His Majesty King George the Third, for New York was in those days still a province of England, they talked over village gossip and told stories. If by chance an old newspaper should fall into their hands from some passing traveler, they would listen as Van Bummel, the schoolmaster, read them its contents, and it would have been worth any statesman's money to hear the discussions that followed. Nicholas Vedder, a patriarch of the village, made his opinions known by the manner in which he smoked his pipe. Short puffs indicated anger; but when he was pleased, he would inhale the smoke slowly and emit it in light and delicate clouds. But even so august a personage could not escape the scolding of Dame Van Winkle when she appeared in search of her husband. One day, seeking to escape the labor of the farm and the clamor of his wife, Rip shouldered his gun and walked high into the Catskills in search of squirrels. All day the mountains echoed and re-echoed with the reports of his gun. Finally he threw himself on a green knoll that looked down into a deep glen, wild and lonely. Rip lay musing on the scene as evening gradually advanced, and sighed as he thought of going home. As he was about to descend, he heard a voice calling, "Rip Van Winkle! Rip Van Winkle!" He perceived a strange figure toiling up the rocks, and bending under the weight of something on his back. He was surprised to see any human being in this lonely place, but supposing it to be one of his neighbors in need of assistance, he hastened down to help. The stranger was a short old fellow with a grizzled beard. His dress was of the antique Dutch fashion and he bore a stout keg that Rip supposed was full of liquor. He made signs for Rip to assist him, and together they clambered up a narrow gully. Every now and then long rolling peals like thunder seemed to issue out of a deep ravine. Passing through this ravine, they came to a hollow that looked like a small amphitheater. In the center was a company of odd-looking persons playing at ninepins. The thunderous noise Rip had heard from afar was the sound of the ball rolling towards the pins. Like Rip's guide, they were dressed in an outlandish fashion, with long knives in their belts and enormous breeches. What seemed particularly odd to Rip was that though these folks were amusing themselves, they maintained the gravest faces, the most mysterious silence, and were, in fact, the most melancholy party he had ever witnessed. They stared at Rip in such a way that his heart turned within him and his knees banged together for fear. Rip's guide emptied the keg into large flagons. The company quaffed the liquor in profound silence and then returned to their game. As Rip's apprehension subsided, he ventured to taste the beverage. One taste provoked another, and at length his senses were overpowered and he fell into a deep sleep. Upon waking, he found himself on the green knoll whence he had first seen the old man. It was a bright sunny morning. "Surely," thought Rip, "I have not slept here all night." He recalled the strange men—"Oh! That wicked flagon!" thought Rip. "What excuse shall I make to Dame Van Winkle?" He looked around for his gun, but found only an old firelock encrusted with rust. Suspecting he had been robbed, he determined to revisit the scene of the previous evening to demand his gun. As he rose to walk, he found himself stiff in the joints. With some difficulty, he found the gully up which he and his companion had ascended, but could find no traces of the ravine that had led to the amphitheater. He shouldered the rusty firelock, and, with a heart full of trouble, turned his steps homeward. As he approached the village he met a number of people, but none whom he knew, which somewhat surprised him, for he had thought himself acquainted with everyone in the country round. Their dress, too, was of a different fashion. They all stared at him with surprise, and stroked their chins. When Rip did the same, he found to his astonishment that his beard had grown a foot long! A troop of children ran at his heels, hooting after him and pointing at his gray beard. There were houses in the village that he had never seen before, with unfamiliar names inscribed over the doors. He began to wonder whether both he and the world around him were bewitched. "That flagon last night," thought he, "has addled my poor head sadly!" With some difficulty he found his own house. The roof had fallen in and the door was off its hinges. He entered and called for his wife and children, but all was silent. He spotted a dog that looked like his own and called out to him, but the dog snarled and showed his teeth. "My own dog has forgotten me," sighed poor Rip. He hastened to the village inn. Before it there now hung a flag adorned with stars and stripes. He recognized on the sign the face of King George, but now the red coat was blue, the head wore a cocked hat, and underneath the figure was printed GENERAL WASHINGTON. There was a crowd of people around the door, but none that Rip knew. He inquired, "Where's Nicholas Vedder?" There was silence, then an old man replied, "Nicholas Vedder! Why he is dead and gone these eighteen years!" "Where's Van Bummel, the schoolmaster?" "He went off to wars, and is now in Congress." Rip's heart sank at hearing of these sad changes. He said in despair, "I'm not myself. I was myself last night, but I fell asleep on the mountain, and everything's changed, and I can't tell who I am!" The bystanders looked at each other in puzzlement. Then a comely woman pressed through the throng. She had a child in her arms, which, frightened by the gray-bearded man's looks, began to cry. "Hush, Rip," cried she, "the old man won't hurt you." The name of the child and the air of the mother awakened a train of recollections in his mind. He caught the mother and child in his arms and said to the woman, "I am your father—young Rip Van Winkle once—old Rip Van Winkle now! Does nobody know poor Rip Van Winkle?" All stood amazed, until an old woman, peering into his face for a moment, exclaimed, "Sure enough! It is Rip Van Winkle! Welcome home again, old neighbor. Why, where have you been these twenty years?" Rip's story was soon told, for the whole twenty years had been to him but as one night. Many were skeptical, but an old man who was well-versed in the local traditions corroborated his story in the most satisfactory manner. He assured the company that the Catskill Mountains had always been haunted by strange beings; that the great discoverer Hendrick Hudson kept a vigil there with his crew of the Half Moon; that his father had once seen them in their old Dutch clothing playing at ninepins in the hollow of the mountain. Rip's daughter took him home to live with her, her mother having died some years before after breaking a blood vessel in a fit of passion. Having arrived at that happy age when a man can be idle with impunity, Rip took his place once more on the bench at the inn door and was reverenced as one of the patriarchs of the village. He used to tell his story to every stranger that arrived. Some doubted the truth of it, but the old Dutch villagers almost universally gave Rip full credit. Even to this day, whenever a thunderstorm comes up on a summer afternoon, they say that Hendrick Hudson and his crew are at their game of ninepins; and it is a common wish of all henpecked husbands in the neighborhood, when life hangs heavy on their hands, that they might have a quieting draft out of Rip Van Winkle's flagon.

Exercise

"In a village in the Catskill Mountains, there lived a simple, good-natured fellow by the name of Rip Van Winkle. He was a kind neighbour, and the children would shout with joy whenever he approached. The great fault in Rip's nature, though, was his aversion to profitable labour. He did not lack diligence or perseverance..."

Rip Van Winkle is depicted as a simple, good natured, kind, approachable, and loved by children but indifferent to material wellbeing. Let us through an analysis of Rip's personal traits examine individual identity and discover oneself.

A. Explore your character and personality

Enumerate your personality traits, abilities, interests, and hobbies.

Identify the attributes that befits you the most and circle them.

Confident	Ambitious	Fun-loving
Compassionate	Bold	Generosus
Honest	Brave	Gentle
Independent	Caring	Hardworking
Empathetic	Clever	Helpful
Good listener	Dynamic	Responsible

Intelligent	Energetic	Reliable
Kind	Enthusiastic	Studious
Supportive	Cheerful	Sensible
Trustworthy	Creative	Sincere
Optimistic	Curious	Tolerant
Courageous	Committed	understanding
Humble	friendly	perceptive
Positive	Faithful	Happy

Identify the aspects you need to develop or improve from the above and prioritize them.

B. Self Assessment

"Your beliefs become your thoughts,
Your thoughts become your words,
Your words become your actions,
Your actions become your habits,
Your habits become your values,
Your values become your destiny."

– Gandhi

Identify from the list given below the values that you consider important to you in life.

Try to rate each value listed with the following scale as per its importance in your life – "1" being not as important and "5" being extremely important.

Values in Life	*Least Important* ➡ *Most Important*				
Family	1	2	3	4	5
Friends	1	2	3	4	5
Good health	1	2	3	4	5
Education	1	2	3	4	5
Spiritual well-being	1	2	3	4	5
Happiness and fun	1	2	3	4	5

Values in Life	*Least Important* ➡ *Most Important*				
Career	1	2	3	4	5
Relaxation and Free time	1	2	3	4	5
discipline and order in life	1	2	3	4	5
Recognition or fame	1	2	3	4	5
Respect for elders	1	2	3	4	5
Social responsibility	1	2	3	4	5
Personal achievement	1	2	3	4	5
Personal Comfort	1	2	3	4	5
Gaining Wealth	1	2	3	4	5

C. Mind map the important people in the story, their significance, and connect their relationship.

The Road Not Taken

Robert Frost

Two roads diverged in a yellow wood,
And sorry I could not travel both
And be one traveler, long I stood
And looked down one as far as I could
To where it bent in the undergrowth;

Then took the other, as just as fair,
And having perhaps the better claim,
Because it was grassy and wanted wear;
Though as for that the passing there
Had worn them really about the same,

And both that morning equally lay
In leaves no step had trodden black.
Oh, I kept the first for another day!
Yet knowing how way leads on to way,
I doubted if I should ever come back.

I shall be telling this with a sigh
Somewhere ages and ages hence:
Two roads diverged in a wood, and I—

I took the one less traveled by,
And that has made all the difference.

Exercise

"Two roads diverged in a wood, and I—
I took the one less traveled by,
And that has made all the difference."

The poet indicates life's choices with the metaphor of the two roads that diverged before him and the anxiety he experienced to choose between the two. The poem is an invitation to overcome hesitation and to forge ahead so as not to regret of not having made a choice at all.

A. Attempt Dialogue writing between two friends on the recent difficult choices they took and the factors that influenced their decisions.

Example:

ALEX: Hey Jordan, how's it going?

JORDAN: Hi Alex! Pretty good. I finally decided about grad school. I'm staying here instead of studying abroad. How about you? How did your job choice turn out?

ALEX: It was tough! I had to choose between a high-paying job in the city and a smaller startup in a different state. I went with the startup. It felt like a better fit for my passions.

JORDAN: That's a big decision. For me, staying close to family and having more networking opportunities won out over the adventure of studying abroad.

ALEX: Yeah, family and career goals play a big role. It sounds like you made a thoughtful choice.

JORDAN: Thanks! And it sounds like you did too. It's all about what aligns best with our long-term goals.

ALEX: Exactly. It's good to talk it out. Thanks for sharing, Jordan.

JORDAN: Anytime, Alex. Here's to making the most of our choices!

ALEX: Cheers to that!

B. Group Discussion: Engage in a discussion on the initial impressions of the poem. What are the central themes? How does the imagery in the poem contribute to its meaning?

1. What were your first thoughts or feelings when you read 'The Road Not Taken'?
   Example: I felt the poem was about the impact of our choices and how we reflect on them.
2. What do you think is the main theme of the poem?
   Example: The theme seems to be about how our choices define us. The speaker reflects on how decisions shape our path in life.
3. How does the imagery, like 'a yellow wood' and 'two roads,' contribute to the poem's meaning?
   Example: The imagery of the 'yellow wood' creates a sense of change and contemplation, setting a reflective mood.

Snake

D.H. Lawrence

A snake came to my water-trough
On a hot, hot day, and I in pyjamas for the heat,
To drink there.

In the deep, strange-scented shade of the great dark carob tree
I came down the steps with my pitcher
And must wait, must stand and wait, for there he was at the
trough before me.

He reached down from a fissure in the earth-wall in the gloom
And trailed his yellow-brown slackness soft-bellied down, over
the edge of the stone trough
And rested his throat upon the stone bottom,
And where the water had dripped from the tap, in a small
clearness,
He sipped with his straight mouth,
Softly drank through his straight gums, into his slack long body,
Silently.

Someone was before me at my water-trough,
And I, like a second-comer, waiting.

He lifted his head from his drinking, as cattle do,
And looked at me vaguely, as drinking cattle do,
And flickered his two-forked tongue from his lips, and mused a moment,
And stooped and drank a little more,
Being earth-brown, earth-golden from the burning bowels of the earth
On the day of Sicilian July, with Etna smoking.

The voice of my education said to me
He must be killed,
For in Sicily the black, black snakes are innocent, the gold are venomous.

And voices in me said, If you were a man
You would take a stick and break him now, and finish him off.

But must I confess how I liked him,
How glad I was he had come like a guest in quiet, to drink at my water-trough
And depart peaceful, pacified, and thankless,
Into the burning bowels of this earth?

Was it cowardice, that I dared not kill him?
Was it perversity, that I longed to talk to him?
Was it humility, to feel so honoured?
I felt so honoured.

And yet those voices:
If you were not afraid, you would kill him!

And truly I was afraid, I was most afraid,
But even so, honoured still more
That he should seek my hospitality
From out the dark door of the secret earth.

He drank enough
And lifted his head, dreamily, as one who has drunken,
And flickered his tongue like a forked night on the air, so black,
Seeming to lick his lips,
And looked around like a god, unseeing, into the air,
And slowly turned his head,
And slowly, very slowly, as if thrice a dream,
Proceeded to draw his slow length curving round
And climb again the broken bank of my wall-face.

And as he put his head into that dreadful hole,
And as he slowly drew up, snake-easing his shoulders, and
entered farther,
A sort of horror, a sort of protest against his withdrawing into
that horrid black hole,
Deliberately going into the blackness, and slowly drawing himself
after,
Overcame me now his back was turned.

I looked round, I put down my pitcher,
I picked up a clumsy log
And threw it at the water-trough with a clatter.

I think it did not hit him,
But suddenly that part of him that was left behind convulsed in an
undignified haste,
Writhed like lightning, and was gone
Into the black hole, the earth-lipped fissure in the wall-front,
At which, in the intense still noon, I stared with fascination.

And immediately I regretted it.
I thought how paltry, how vulgar, what a mean act!
I despised myself and the voices of my accursed human education.

And I thought of the albatross,
And I wished he would come back, my snake.

For he seemed to me again like a king,
Like a king in exile, uncrowned in the underworld,
Now due to be crowned again.

And so, I missed my chance with one of the lords
Of life.
And I have something to expiate:
A pettiness.

Exercise

"For he seemed to me again like a king,
Like a king in exile, uncrowned in the underworld,
Now due to be crowned again"

The snake is generally known as a sly creature and is synonymous with sin and evil but the poet recognizes him as worthy of honour being majestic and is overcome with regret for the harm he intended to do. The poet deals with the 'tension of opposites' as he tries to come to terms with the human beings stealing away the dignity endowed by the creator on the reptiles.

A. Narrative writing

Rewrite D.H. Lawrence's "Snake" as a fairytale, preserving the poem's emotional and thematic essence, while integrating imaginative and magical aspects into the story.

For Example:

Title: The Serpent's Visit

On a sweltering summer afternoon, farmer Thomas worked in his garden, surrounded by vibrant flowers and ancient trees. As he toiled near an old well, he noticed a shimmering snake with scales that glittered like stars. It coiled gracefully under the well's shadow, casting a soft, golden glow.

Thomas's initial fear melted away as he saw the snake's eyes, which sparkled with an otherworldly light. The serpent drank from the well, and as it did, the water began to shimmer with a rainbow of colours, casting magical patterns across the garden.

Feeling a mix of awe and guilt, Thomas watched as the snake's presence seemed to breathe life into the garden. Flowers bloomed more brilliantly, and the air was filled with a sweet, enchanting fragrance. The snake, with its serene gaze, seemed to be a guardian of nature's hidden magic.

As the serpent slithered away, leaving behind a trail of glimmering dust, Thomas felt a profound connection to the mystical world around him. The encounter had opened his eyes to the magic that lay beyond the ordinary, teaching him to cherish and respect the wonders of nature.

From that day forward, Thomas tended his garden with a renewed sense of wonder, always remembering the magical visit of the serpent.

B. Creative writing

Write a creative dialogue between yourself and the snake, exploring themes of fear, admiration, and human-animal interaction.

For Example:

THOMAS: (*nervously, but intrigued*) "Hello there. I didn't expect to see a snake like you. Your scales are beautiful. Why are you here?"

SNAKE: (*calmly*) "Hello, Thomas. I'm here to show you that there's beauty in things we don't understand. Your sense of wonder is lovely, but learning to understand is even better."

THOMAS: (*hesitant*) "I've always been taught to be afraid of snakes. How do I get past that fear?"

SNAKE: (*slithering closer*) "Fear comes from not knowing. When you admire and try to understand, you find peace. We're not so different—both of us live in this world and seek a place in it."

THOMAS: (*smiling slightly*) "I see. Your visit has made me rethink things."

SNAKE: (*with a gentle nod*) "That's the idea. Embrace the mystery and learn from it. Respect and understanding bring magic."

THOMAS: (*with gratitude*) "Thank you. I'll remember your words. Goodbye, and take care."

SNAKE: (*slithering away, leaving a trail of sparkling dust*) "Goodbye, Thomas. May your garden and your heart grow with wonder."

The Lady or the Tiger

Frank Stockton

In the very olden time there lived a semi-barbaric king, whose ideas, though somewhat polished and sharpened by the progressiveness of distant Latin neighbors, were still large, florid, and untrammeled, as became the half of him which was barbaric. He was a man of exuberant fancy, and, withal, of an authority so irresistible that, at his will, he turned his varied fancies into facts. He was greatly given to self-communing, and, when he and himself agreed upon anything, the thing was done. When every member of his domestic and political systems moved smoothly in its appointed course, his nature was bland and genial; but, whenever there was a little hitch, and some of his orbs got out of their orbits, he was blander and more genial still, for nothing pleased him so much as to make the crooked straight and crush down uneven places.

Among the borrowed notions by which his barbarism had become semified was that of the public arena, in which, by exhibitions of manly and beastly valor, the minds of his subjects were refined and cultured.

But even here the exuberant and barbaric fancy asserted itself. The arena of the king was built, not to give the people an opportunity of hearing the rhapsodies of dying gladiators, nor to enable them to view the inevitable conclusion of a conflict between religious opinions and hungry jaws, but for purposes far better adapted to widen and develop the mental energies of the people. This vast amphitheater, with its encircling galleries, its mysterious vaults, and its unseen passages, was an agent of poetic justice, in which crime was punished, or virtue rewarded, by the decrees of an impartial and incorruptible chance.girlplays

When a subject was accused of a crime of sufficient importance to interest the king, public notice was given that on an appointed day the fate of the accused person would be decided in the king›s arena, a structure which well deserved its name, for, although its form and plan were borrowed from afar, its purpose emanated solely from the brain of this man, who, every barleycorn a king, knew no tradition to which he owed more allegiance than pleased his fancy, and who ingrafted on every adopted form of human thought and action the rich growth of his barbaric idealism.

When all the people had assembled in the galleries, and the king, surrounded by his court, sat high up on his throne of royal state on one side of the arena, he gave a signal, a door beneath him opened, and the accused subject stepped out into the amphitheater. Directly opposite him, on the other side of the enclosed space, were two doors, exactly alike and side by side. It was the duty and the privilege of the person on trial to walk directly to these doors and open one of them. He could open either door he pleased; he was subject to no guidance or influence but that of the aforementioned impartial and incorruptible chance. If he opened the one, there came out of it a hungry tiger, the fiercest and most cruel that could be procured, which immediately sprang upon him and tore him to pieces as a punishment for his guilt. The moment that the case of the criminal was thus decided, doleful iron bells were clanged, great wails went up from the hired mourners posted on the outer rim of the arena, and the vast audience, with bowed heads and downcast hearts, wended slowly their homeward way, mourning greatly that one so young and fair, or so old and respected, should have merited so dire a fate.

But, if the accused person opened the other door, there came forth from it a lady, the most suitable to his years and station that his majesty could select among his fair subjects, and to this lady he was immediately married, as a reward of his innocence. It mattered not that he might already possess a wife and family, or that his affections might be engaged upon an object of his own selection; the king allowed no such subordinate arrangements to interfere with his great scheme of retribution and reward. The exercises, as in the other instance, took place immediately, and in the arena. Another door opened beneath the king, and a priest, followed by a band of choristers, and dancing maidens blowing joyous airs on golden horns and treading an epithalamic measure, advanced to where the pair stood, side by side, and the wedding was promptly and cheerily solemnized. Then the gay brass bells rang forth their merry peals, the people shouted glad hurrahs, and the innocent man, preceded by children strewing flowers on his path, led his bride to his home.

This was the king›s semi-barbaric method of administering justice. Its perfect fairness is obvious. The criminal could not know out of which door would come the lady; he opened either he pleased, without having the slightest idea whether, in the next instant, he was to be devoured or married. On some occasions the tiger came out of one door, and on some out of the other. The decisions of this tribunal were not only fair, they were positively determinate: the accused person was instantly punished if he found himself guilty, and, if innocent, he was rewarded on the spot, whether he liked it or not. There was no escape from the judgments of the king's arena.

The institution was a very popular one. When the people gathered together on one of the great trial days, they never knew whether they were to witness a bloody slaughter or a hilarious wedding. This element of uncertainty lent an interest to the occasion which it could not otherwise have attained. Thus, the masses were entertained and pleased, and the thinking part of the community could bring no charge of unfairness against this plan, for did not the accused person have the whole matter in his own hands?

This semi-barbaric king had a daughter as blooming as his most florid fancies, and with a soul as fervent and imperious as his own. As is usual in such cases, she was the apple of his eye, and was loved by him above all humanity. Among his courtiers was a young man of that fineness of blood and lowness of station common to the conventional heroes of romance who love royal maidens. This royal maiden was well satisfied with her lover, for he was handsome and brave to a degree unsurpassed in all this kingdom, and she loved him with an ardor that had enough of barbarism in it to make it exceedingly warm and strong. This love affair moved on happily for many months, until one day the king happened to discover its existence. He did not hesitate nor waver in regard to his duty in the premises. The youth was immediately cast into prison, and a day was appointed for his trial in the king's arena. This, of course, was an especially important occasion, and his majesty, as well as all the people, was greatly interested in the workings and development of this trial. Never before had such a case occurred; never before had a subject dared to love the daughter of the king. In after years such things became commonplace enough, but then they were in no slight degree novel and startling.

The tiger-cages of the kingdom were searched for the most savage and relentless beasts, from which the fiercest monster might be selected for the arena; and the ranks of maiden youth and beauty throughout the land were carefully surveyed by competent judges in order that the young man might have a fitting bride in case fate did not determine for him a different destiny. Of course, everybody knew that the deed with which the accused was charged had been done. He had loved the princess, and neither he, she, nor any one else, thought of denying the fact; but the king would not think of allowing any fact of this kind to interfere with the workings of the tribunal, in which he took such great delight and satisfaction. No matter how the affair turned out, the youth would be disposed of, and the king would take an aesthetic pleasure in watching the course of events, which would determine whether or not the young man had done wrong in allowing himself to love the princess.

The appointed day arrived. From far and near the people gathered, and thronged the great galleries of the arena, and crowds, unable to gain admittance, massed themselves against its outside walls. The king and his court were in their places, opposite the twin doors, those fateful portals, so terrible in their similarity.

All was ready. The signal was given. A door beneath the royal party opened, and the lover of the princess walked into the arena. Tall, beautiful, fair, his appearance was greeted with a low hum of admiration and anxiety. Half the audience had not known so grand a youth had lived among them. No wonder the princess loved him! What a terrible thing for him to be there!

As the youth advanced into the arena he turned, as the custom was, to bow to the king, but he did not think at all of that royal personage. His eyes were fixed upon the princess, who sat to the right of her father. Had it not been for the moiety of barbarism in her nature it is probable that lady would not have been there, but her intense and fervid soul would not allow her to be absent on an occasion in which she was so terribly interested. From the moment that the decree had gone forth that her lover should decide his fate in the king's arena, she had thought of nothing, night or day, but this great event and the various subjects connected with it. Possessed of more power, influence, and force of character than any one who had ever before been interested in such a case, she had done what no other person had done – she had possessed herself of the secret of the doors. She knew in which of the two rooms, that lay behind those doors, stood the cage of the tiger, with its open front, and in which waited the lady. Through these thick doors, heavily curtained with skins on the inside, it was impossible that any noise or suggestion should come from within to the person who should approach to raise the latch of one of them. But gold, and the power of a woman's will, had brought the secret to the princess.

And not only did she know in which room stood the lady ready to emerge, all blushing and radiant, should her door be opened, but she knew who the lady was. It was one of the fairest and loveliest of the damsels of the court who had been selected as the reward of the accused youth, should he be proved innocent of the crime of aspiring to one so far above him; and the princess hated her. Often had she seen, or imagined that she had seen, this fair creature throwing glances of admiration upon the person of her lover, and sometimes she thought these glances were perceived, and even returned. Now and then she had seen them talking together; it was but for a moment or two, but much can be said in a brief space; it may have been on most unimportant topics, but how could she know that? The girl was lovely, but she had dared to raise her eyes to the loved one of the princess; and, with all the intensity of the savage blood transmitted to her through long lines of wholly barbaric ancestors, she hated the woman who blushed and trembled behind that silent door.

When her lover turned and looked at her, and his eye met hers as she sat there, paler and whiter than any one in the vast ocean of anxious faces about her, he saw, by that power of quick perception which is given to those whose souls are one, that she knew behind which door crouched the tiger, and behind which stood the lady. He had expected her to know it. He understood her nature, and his soul was assured that she would never rest until she had made plain to herself this thing, hidden to all other lookers-on, even to the king. The only hope for the youth in which there was any element of certainty was based upon the success of the princess in discovering this mystery; and the moment he looked upon her, he saw she had succeeded, as in his soul he knew she would succeed.

Then it was that his quick and anxious glance asked the question: «Which?» It was as plain to her as if he shouted it from where he stood. There was not an instant to be lost. The question was asked in a flash; it must be answered in another.

Her right arm lay on the cushioned parapet before her. She raised her hand, and made a slight, quick movement toward the right. No one but her lover saw her. Every eye but his was fixed on the man in the arena.

He turned, and with a firm and rapid step he walked across the empty space. Every heart stopped beating, every breath was held, every eye was fixed immovably upon that man. Without the slightest hesitation, he went to the door on the right, and opened it.

Now, the point of the story is this: Did the tiger come out of that door, or did the lady ?

The more we reflect upon this question, the harder it is to answer. It involves a study of the human heart which leads us through devious mazes of passion, out of which it is difficult to find our way. Think of it, fair reader, not as if the decision of the question depended upon yourself, but upon that hot-blooded, semi-barbaric princess, her soul at a white heat beneath the combined fires of despair and jealousy. She had lost him, but who should have him?

How often, in her waking hours and in her dreams, had she started in wild horror, and covered her face with her hands as she thought of her lover opening the door on the other side of which waited the cruel fangs of the tiger!

But how much oftener had she seen him at the other door! How in her grievous reveries had she gnashed her teeth, and torn her hair, when she saw his start of rapturous delight as he opened the door of the lady! How her soul had burned in agony when she had seen him rush to meet that woman, with her flushing cheek and sparkling eye of triumph; when she had seen him lead her forth, his whole frame kindled with the joy of recovered life; when she had heard the glad shouts from the multitude, and the wild ringing of the happy bells; when she had seen the priest, with his joyous followers, advance to the couple, and make them man and wife before her very eyes; and when she had seen them walk away together upon their path of flowers, followed by the tremendous shouts of the hilarious multitude, in which her one despairing shriek was lost and drowned!

Would it not be better for him to die at once, and go to wait for her in the blessed regions of semi-barbaric futurity?

And yet, that awful tiger, those shrieks, that blood!

Her decision had been indicated in an instant, but it had been made after days and nights of anguished deliberation. She had known she would be asked, she had decided what she would answer, and, without the slightest hesitation, she had moved her hand to the right.

The question of her decision is one not to be lightly considered, and it is not for me to presume to set myself up as the one person able to answer it. And so I leave it with all of you: Which came out of the opened door – the lady, or the tiger?

Exercise

**"Now, the point of the story is this:
Did the tiger come out of that door, or did the lady?
The more we reflect upon this question,
the harder it is to answer. It involves a study of
the human heart which leads us through devious mazes of
passion, out of which it is difficult to find our way."**

The story *The Lady, or the Tiger* is noted for its ambiguous ending impels us to learn the art of Problem solving as a valuable skill in personal and professional life, to navigate challenges, make better decisions and achieve goals.

A. **Problem Solving:**
Problem solving is the process of identifying and analyzing the complex situations and achieving a goal by overcoming obstacles.

Problem solving involves:

- Critical thinking
- Creativity
- Logical reasoning
- Decision-making
- Resilience
- Communication
- Adaptability

Solving a Problem

Lily: Hey, Emma. I'm really struggling to make this decision. I don't know what to do.

Emma: What's your problem? Tell me.

Lily: I just got a job offer in the different state, it means leaving my family and friends behind. I don't know if it's worth it.

Emma: That's tough. What are your priorities? What's most important to you?

LILY: I guess I want to advance my career, but I also value my relationships. I don't want to lose those connections.

EMMA: Okay, let's discuss on it. What are the pros and cons of taking the job?

LILY: Well, the pros are career advancement, new experiences, and a higher salary. But the cons are leaving loved ones behind, starting over, and uncertainty.

EMMA: That helps in clarifying things. Now, what are your non-negotiables? What do you need to feel happy and fulfilled?

LILY: I need to feel connected to my loved ones, pursue my passions, and have a sense of community.

EMMA: Okay, so how can you achieve those non-negotiables in either scenario? Whether you take the job or stay, how can you make it work?

LILY: If I take the job, I could schedule regular video calls with family and friends, join local groups to build a new community, and pursue hobbies in my free time.

EMMA: Exactly! And if you stay, how can you still advance your career and pursue your passions?

LILY: I could take on new projects, attend local conferences, and seek out mentorship opportunities.

EMMA: See, there are solutions to both scenarios. It's not a perfect choice, but which one aligns more with your values and priorities?

LILY: I think I need to take the job. It's scary, but it feels right for my career and personal growth.

EMMA: That's great! Remember, life is full of trade-offs. But by prioritizing what matters most, you'll make the best decision for yourself.

Draft a problem solving scenarios of the problems below:

1. A family member's behavior is causing tension during gatherings. How do you address the issue?
2. A close friend is struggling with a personal issue and turns to you for help. How do you support them?

B. Solve the scrambled word puzzle:

1. nloed ________________
2. rcarbirab ________________
3. slgeilare ________________
4. dhrsaipose ________________
5. stiuntionti ________________
6. hentipsunm ________________
7. ehttaerpmiha ________________
8. latirpmai ________________
9. almirnic ________________
10. desucca ________________

How Frog Went to Heaven: A Tale of Angola

Aaron Shepard

There was a young man named Kimana. He wanted to marry the Sky Maiden. He wrote a letter to her father, the Sun Chief.

Kimana went to Rabbit. "Will you take this letter?"

Rabbit said, "I cannot go to Heaven."

Kimana went to Antelope. "Will you take this letter?"

Antelope said, "I cannot go to Heaven."

Kimana went to Hawk. "Will you take this letter?"

Hawk said, "I can go halfway. But I cannot go to Heaven."

Then Frog came to Kimana. "Why do you not take the letter yourself?"

Kimana said, "This I cannot do."

Frog said, "Then I will take it for you."

Kimana laughed. "Can a frog take a letter to Heaven?"

Frog said, "Whatever it is, I can do it. But only if I try."

Now, Frog lived by a well. Every day, the girls who served the Sun Chief came to this well. They climbed down from Heaven on a web made by Spider. Then they filled their water jugs and went home.

Frog put the letter in his mouth and hid in the well. The girls from Heaven came for water, singing their song.

Good day to you, my sister.
Good day to you.

They lowered their jugs into the well, and Frog jumped into one. The girls did not see.

Then the girls climbed back up the web of Spider. They went into the house of the Sun Chief and left the jugs in a room.

Frog was alone. He jumped out of the jug and spit the letter out on a bench. Then he hid in a corner.

The Sun Chief came for a drink of water. He saw the letter and opened it. He read, "I, Kimana, a man of earth, wish to marry the Sky Maiden, your daughter."

The Sun Chief said, "How can this be?"

He went to the girls who fetched water. "Did you bring this letter?"

The girls said, "We did not."

He went to his wife, the Moon Lady, and read it to her. "What should we do?"

The Moon Lady said, "Don't ask me! Ask your daughter!"

He went to his daughter. The Sky Maiden said, "Let us see if he can bring a wedding gift."

So the Sun Chief wrote a letter and set it on the bench. Then he went away.

Frog came out and put the letter in his mouth. Then he climbed into an empty jug.

The next day, the girls took the jugs and climbed down to earth, singing their song.

Good day to you, my sister.
Good day to you.

They lowered their jugs into the well, and Frog jumped out. The girls did not see.

Then the girls went back to Heaven.

Frog took the letter to Kimana, and Kimana read it. "You may marry my daughter if you bring a purse of money."

Kimana said, "This I cannot do."

Frog said, "Then I will bring it for you."

Kimana laughed. "You took a letter to Heaven. But can you bring a purse of money?"

Frog said, "Whatever it is, I can do it. But only if I try."

Kimana gave Frog a purse of money. Frog took hold of it with his mouth and carried it to the well. He climbed in and waited.

The girls from Heaven came to the well.

Good day to you, my sister.
Good day to you.

Frog got into one of the jugs. The girls returned to Heaven and left him in the room.

Frog set the money on the bench. Then he hid.

The Sun Chief came and found the purse. "How can this be?"

He went to the girls. "Did you bring this money?"

The girls said, "We did not."

He went to his wife. The Moon Lady said, "Don't ask me! Ask your daughter!"

He went to his daughter. The Sky Maiden said, "Let us see if he can come fetch me."

So the Sun Chief wrote a letter and left it on the bench.

Frog put the letter in his mouth and climbed into an empty jug. The next day, the girls carried him to earth.

Good day to you, my sister.
Good day to you.

He jumped back into the well, and the girls went back to Heaven.

Frog brought the letter to Kimana, and Kimana read it. "You may marry my daughter if you come and fetch her."

Kimana said, "This I cannot do."

Frog said, "Then I will fetch her for you."

Kimana laughed. "You took a letter to Heaven. You brought a purse of money. But can you fetch a bride?"

Frog said, "Whatever it is, I can do it. But only if I try."

Frog climbed back into the well. The girls came with their jugs.

Good day to you, my sister.
Good day to you.

They carried him to Heaven.

Frog jumped out. He spit in all the jugs of water. *Ptui. Ptui. Ptui.* Then he hid in an empty jug.

The people of the house came and drank the water. They all got sick.

The Sun Chief called for the spirit doctor. The doctor told him, "You promised your daughter to a man of earth, but she has not gone. He has sent an evil spirit with a sickness. The evil spirit is in the shape of a frog."

The Sun Chief went to his wife. The Moon Lady said, "Don't ask me! Ask your daughter!"

He went to his daughter. The Sky Maiden said, "I will go."

The next day, the Sky Maiden went with the girls down to the well.

Good day to you, my sister.
Good day to you.

The girls filled their jugs, and Frog jumped out. Then the girls left the Sky Maiden and went home.

Frog jumped out of the well. "I will lead you to your husband."

The Sky Maiden laughed. "Can a frog lead a woman?"

Frog said, "I took a letter to Heaven. I brought a purse of money. I fetched a bride. Whatever it was, I could do it. But only since I tried."

The Sky Maiden said, "Then it is you I will marry."

She took Frog back to Heaven and married him. They lived on and on.

And Kimana is still waiting for his bride.

Exercise

"Frog said, "I took a letter to Heaven.
I brought a purse of money. I fetched a bride.
Whatever it was, I could do it. But only since I tried."

This whimsical tale adapted from 'Tales of Angola' titled "The Son of Kimanaueze and the Daughter of Sun and Moon," belongs to the Mbaka tribe, part of the Ambundu people of northwest Angola. Kimanaueze known in the story as "Kimana" is a common figure in Ambundu stories.

In African countries it is customary for a groom to give a gift to the bride's family commonly known as "wooing present," "bride-price," and "bride-wealth."

A. Letter Writing:

Attempt the task given below:

Task: Write a letter to a Newspaper Editor about the faulty street lights in your area.

B. Persuasive Dialogue

Presenting arguments and counter arguments effectively. Here's a basic outline for a persuasive dialogue:

1. **Introduction**

   Participant 1 (P1): Presents the main argument or viewpoint.

   Participant 2 (P2): Acknowledges the viewpoint and presents an opposing or neutral stance.

2. **Argument Presentation**

   P1: Provides supporting evidence and reasoning for their viewpoint.

   P2: Raises questions or concerns about the argument, highlighting potential weaknesses or alternative perspectives.

3. **Counter argument and Rebuttal**

   P1: Addresses P2's concerns, providing counterarguments and reinforcing the original position with additional evidence or clarification.

   P2: Offers additional counterpoints or questions to test the strength of P1's rebuttal.

4. **Resolution**

   P1: Summarizes the key points, reiterates the strength of their argument, and suggests a course of action or a compromise.

   P2: Reflects on the discussion, possibly agreeing with some points or suggesting further considerations.

Example – Persuasive Dialogue:

- **Introduction:**

  P1: "I believe that we should implement a four-day workweek. It's been shown to increase productivity and improve employee satisfaction."

  P2: "I see your point, but I'm concerned that a shorter workweek might disrupt business operations and reduce overall output."

- **Argument Presentation:**

  P1: "Studies from various countries have demonstrated that employees working four days a week are more focused and efficient. For example, Microsoft Japan reported a 40% increase in productivity after adopting a four-day workweek."

  P2: "That's interesting, but what about industries that require constant coverage or have tight deadlines? A shorter week might lead to delays or operational challenges."

- **Counterargument and Rebuttal:**

  P1: "In industries with constant coverage needs, the model can be adapted. For instance, rotating shifts or flexible schedules can ensure coverage without the traditional five-day week. Moreover, companies that have adopted this model report that employees work more efficiently during their shorter hours."

  P2: "Even with adaptations, there might be an initial period of adjustment and potential resistance from both employees and management."

- **Resolution:**

  P1: "The initial adjustment period is a valid concern, but the long-term benefits, including higher employee morale and reduced burnout, make it worthwhile. Implementing pilot programs could be a way to test this model without fully committing right away."

  P2: "I can see the potential benefits. Perhaps starting with a pilot program could address the concerns and provide data to make a more informed decision."

Task: Using the given example write a conversation about the habit of reading books.

The Scribe

Kristin Hunter

We been living in the apartment over the Silver Dollar Check Cashing Service five years. But I never had any reason to go in there till two days ago, when Mom had to go to the Wash-a-Mat and asked me to get some change. And man! Are those people who come in there in some bad shape. Old man Silver and old man Dollar, who own the place, have signs tacked up everywhere: NO LOUNGING, NO LOITERING THIS IS NOT A WAITING ROOM and MINIMUM CHECK CASHING FEE, 50¢ and LETTERS ADDRESSED, 50¢ and LETTERS READ, 75¢ and LETTERS WRITTEN, ONE DOLLAR And everybody who comes in there to cash a check gets their picture taken like they're some kind of criminal. After I got my change, I stood around for a while digging the action. First comes an old lady with some kind of long form to fill out. The mean old man behind the counter points to the "One Dollar" sign. She nods. So he starts to fill it out for her. "Name?" "Muskogee Marie Lawson." "SPELL it!" he hollers. "M, m, u, s—well, I don't exactly know, sir." "I'll put it down 'Marie,' then. Age?" "Sixty-three my last birthday." "Date of birth?" "March twenty-third"—a pause—"I think, 1900."

"Look, Marie," he says, which makes me mad, hearing him first-name a dignified old gray-haired lady like that, "if you'd been born in 1900, you'd be seventy-two. Either I put that down, or I put 1910." "Whatever you think best, sir," she says timidly. He sighs, rolls his eyes to the ceiling, and bangs his fist on the form angrily. Then he fills out the rest. "One dollar," he says when he's finished. She pays like she's grateful to him for taking the trouble.

Next is a man with a cane, a veteran who has to let the government know he moved. He wants old man Silver to do this for him, but he doesn't want him to know he can't do it himself. "My eyes are kind of bad, sir. Will you fill this thing out for me? Tell them I moved from 121 South 15th Street to 203 North Decatur Street." Old man Silver doesn't blink an eye. Just fills out the form, and charges the crippled man a dollar. And it goes on like that. People who can't read or write or count their change. People who don't know how to pay their gas bills, don't know how to fill out forms, don't know how to address envelopes. And old man Silver and old man Dollar cleaning up on all of them. It's pitiful. It's disgusting. Makes me so mad I want to yell. And I do, but mostly at Mom. "Mom, did you know there are hundreds of people in this city who can't read and write?" Mom isn't upset. She's a wise woman. "Of course, James," she says. "A lot of the older people around here haven't had your advantages. They came from down South, and they had to quit school very young to go to work.

"In the old days, nobody cared whether our people got an education. They were only interested in getting the crops in." She sighed. "Sometimes I think they still don't care. If we hadn't gotten you into that good school, you might not be able to read so well either. A lot of boys and girls your age can't, you know." "But that's awful!" I say. "How do they expect us to make it in a big city? You can't even cross the streets if you can't read the 'Walk' and 'Don't Walk' signs." "It's hard," Mom says, "but the important thing to remember is it's no disgrace. There was a time in history when nobody could read or write except a special class of people." And Mom takes down her Bible. She has three Bible study certificates and is always giving me lessons from Bible history. I don't exactly go for all the stuff she believes in, but sometimes it is interesting. "In ancient times," she says, "no one could read or write except a special class of people known as scribes. It was their job to write down the laws given by the rabbis and the judges. No one else could do it. "Jesus criticized the scribes," she goes on, "because they were so proud of themselves. But he needed them to write down his teachings." "Man," I said when she finished, "that's something." My mind was working double time. I'm the best reader and writer in our class. Also it was summertime. I had nothing much to do except go to the park or hang around the library and read till my eyeballs were ready to fall out, and I was tired of doing both.

So the next morning, after my parents went to work, I took Mom's card table and a folding chair down to the sidewalk. I lettered a sign with a Magic Marker, and I was in business. My sign said: PUBLIC SCRIBE—ALL SERVICES FREE I set my table up in front of the Silver Dollar and waited for business. Only one thing bothered me. If the people couldn't read, how would they know what I was there for? But five minutes had hardly passed when an old lady stopped and asked me to read her grandson's letter. She explained that she had just broken her glasses. I knew she was fibbing, but I kept quiet. I read the grandson's letter. It said he was having a fine time in California but was a little short. He would send her some money as soon as he made another payday. I handed the letter back to her. "Thank you, son," she said, and gave me a quarter. I handed that back to her too. The word got around. By noontime I had a whole crowd of customers around my table. I was kept busy writing letters, addressing envelopes, filling out forms, and explaining official-looking letters that scared people half to death. I didn't blame them. The language in some of those letters—"Establish whether your disability is one-fourth, one-third, one-half, or total, and substantiate in paragraph 3 (b) below"—would upset anybody. I mean, why can't the government write English like everybody else? Most of my customers were old, but there were a few young ones too. Like the girl who had gotten a letter about her baby from the Health Service and didn't know what immunization meant. At noontime one old lady brought me some iced tea and a peach, and another gave me some fried chicken wings. I was really having a good time when the shade of all the people standing around me suddenly vanished. The sun hit me like a ton of hot bricks. Only one long shadow fell across my table. The shadow of a tall, heavy, blue-eyed cop. In our neighborhood, when they see a cop, people scatter. That was why the back of my neck was burning.

"What are you trying to do here, sonny?" the cop asks. "Help people out," I tell him calmly, though my knees are knocking together under the table. "Well, you know," he says, "Mr. Silver and Mr. Dollar have been in business a long time on this corner. They are very respected men in this neighborhood. Are you trying to run them out of business?" "I'm not charging anybody," I pointed out. "That," the cop says, "is exactly what they don't like. Mr. Silver says he is glad to have some help with the letter writing. Mr. Dollar says it's only a nuisance to them anyway and takes up too much time. But if you don't charge for your services, it's unfair competition." Well, why not? I thought. After all, I could use a little profit. "All right then," I tell him, "I'll charge a quarter." "Then it is my duty to warn you," the cop says, "that it's against the law to conduct a business without a license. The first time you accept a fee, I'll close you up and run you off this corner." He really had me there. What did I know about licenses? I'm only thirteen, after all. Suddenly I didn't feel like the big black businessman anymore. I felt like a little kid who wanted to holler for his mother. But she was at work, and so was Daddy.

"I'll leave," I said, and did, with all the cool I could muster. But inside I was burning up, and not from the sun. One little old lady hollered "You big bully!" and shook her umbrella at the cop. But the rest of those people were so beaten down they didn't say anything. Just shuffled back on inside to give Mr. Silver and Mr. Dollar their hard-earned money like they always did. I was so mad I didn't know what to do with myself that afternoon. I couldn't watch TV. It was all soap operas anyway, and they seemed dumber than ever. The library didn't appeal to me either. It's not air-conditioned, and the day was hot and muggy. Finally I went to the park and threw stones at the swans in the lake. I was careful not to hit them, but they made good targets because they were so fat and white. Then after a while the sun got lower. I kind of cooled off and came to my senses. They were just big dumb, beautiful birds and not my enemies. I threw them some crumbs from my sandwich and went home. "Daddy," I asked that night, "how come you and Mom never cash checks downstairs in the Silver Dollar?" "Because," he said, "we have an account at the bank, where they cash our checks free." "Well, why doesn't everybody do that?" I wanted to know. "Because some people want all their money right away," he said. "The bank insists that you leave them a minimum balance." "How much?" I asked him. "Only five dollars." "But that five dollars still belongs to you after you leave it there?" "Sure," he says. "And if it's in a savings account, it earns interest."

"So why can't people see they lose money when they pay to have their checks cashed?" "A lot of our people," Mom said, "are scared of banks, period. Some of them remember the Depression, when all the banks closed and the people couldn't get their money out. And others think banks are only for white people. They think they'll be insulted, or maybe even arrested, if they go in there."

Wow. The more I learned, the more pitiful it was. "Are there any black people working at our bank?" "There didn't use to be," Mom said, "but now they have Mr. Lovejoy and Mrs. Adams. You know Mrs. Adams, she's nice. She has a daughter your age." "Hmmm," I said, and shut up before my folks started to wonder why I was asking all those questions. The next morning, when the Silver Dollar opened, I was right there. I hung around near the door, pretending to read a copy of Jet magazine. "Psst," I said to each person who came in. "I know where you can cash checks free." It wasn't easy convincing them. A man blinked his red eyes at me like he didn't believe he had heard right. A carpenter with tools hanging all around his belt said he was on his lunch hour and didn't have time. And a big fat lady with two shopping bags pushed past me and almost knocked me down, she was in such a hurry to give Mr. Silver and Mr. Dollar her money. But finally I had a little group who were interested. It wasn't much. Just three people. Two men—one young, one old— and the little old lady who'd asked me to read her the letter from California. Seemed the grandson had made his payday and sent her a money order. "How far is this place?" asked the young man. "Not far. Just six blocks," I told him. "Aw shoot. I ain't walking all that way just to save fifty cents."

So then I only had two. I was careful not to tell them where we were going. When we finally got to the Establishment Trust National Bank, I said, "This is the place." "I ain't goin' in there," said the old man. "No sir. Not me. You ain't gettin' me in there." And he walked away quickly, going back in the direction where we had come. To tell the truth, the bank did look kind of scary. It was a big building with tall white marble pillars. A lot of Brink's armored trucks and Cadillacs were parked out front. Uniformed guards walked back and forth inside with guns. It might as well have a "Colored Keep Out" sign. Whereas the Silver Dollar is small and dark and funky and dirty. It has trash on the floors and tape across the broken windows. I looked at the little old lady. She smiled back bravely. "Well, we've come this far, son," she said. "Let's not turn back now." So I took her inside. Fortunately Mrs. Adams's window was near the front. "Hi, James," she said. "I've brought you a customer," I told her. Mrs. Adams took the old lady to a desk to fill out some forms. They were gone a long time, but finally they came back. "Now, when you have more business with the bank, Mrs. Franklin, you bring it to me," Mrs. Adams said. "I'll do that," the old lady said. She held out her shiny new bankbook. "Son, do me a favor and read that to me."

"Mrs. Minnie Franklin," I read aloud. "July 9, 1972. Thirty-seven dollars." "That sounds real nice," Mrs. Franklin said. "I guess now I have a bankbook, I'll have to get me some glasses." Mrs. Adams winked at me over the old lady's head, and I winked back. "Do you want me to walk you home?" I asked Mrs. Franklin. "No thank you, son," she said. "I can cross streets by myself all right. I know red from green." And then she winked at both of us, letting us know she knew what was happening. "Son," she went on, "don't ever be afraid to try a thing just because you've never done it before. I took a bus up here from Alabama by myself forty-four years ago. I ain't thought once about going back. But I've stayed too long in one neighborhood since I've been in this city. Now I think I'll go out and take a look at this part of town." Then she was gone. But she had really started me thinking. If an old lady like that wasn't afraid to go in a bank and open an account for the first time in her life, why should I be afraid to go up to City Hall and apply for a license? Wonder how much they charge you to be a scribe?

Exercise

"...don't ever be afraid to try a thing just because you've never done it before."

The story carries forth a powerful message on the importance of education and knowledge bringing to light the struggles of people who cannot read or write. It is also an inspiration to commit to bring forth change in society despite setbacks and challenges.

A. Design a Poster

- Illustrate an innovative idea that you tried to solve a problem.
- Depict a situation where telling the truth builds trust and prevents a misunderstanding.

B. Filling in a Form

Filling in forms is one of the life skills. Here are some examples of forms that you might have to fill as a student: library membership forms, gym membership forms, medical forms, club membership forms. The purpose of filling in forms is to provide information to institutions. Moreover, the information is usually registered in a clear, orderly and easy format:

Fill in the following form:

Regency Literary Club Application for Membership (Use block letters)

First Name: ______________ Surname: ______________

Title: Mr. ❑ Mrs. ❑ Miss ❑

Address: ______________________________

____

Contact Number: ______________________________

DOB: ______________________________

I am applying for membership of Regency Literary Club.

I agree to abide by the rules of Regency Literary Club. I declare that the information given above is true and correct to the best of my knowledge.

Signature: ____________

Date: ________________

How I Taught My Grandmother to Read

Sudha Murty

When I was a girl of about twelve, I used to stay in a village in north Karnataka with my grandparents. Those days, the transport system was not very good, so we used to get the morning paper only in the afternoon. The weekly magazine used to come one day late. All of us would wait eagerly for the bus, which used to come with the papers, weekly magazines and the post. At that time, Triveni was a very popular writer in the Kannada language. She was a wonderful writer. Her style was easy to read and very convincing. Her stories usually dealt with complex psychological problems in the lives of ordinary people and were always very interesting. Unfortunately for Kannada literature, she died very young. Even now, after forty years, people continue to appreciate her novels. One of her novels, called Kashi Yatre, was appearing as a serial in the Kannada weekly Karmaveera then. It is the story of an old lady and her ardent desire to go to Kashi or Varanasi. Most Hindus believe that going to Kashi and worshipping Lord Vishweshvara is the ultimate punya. This old lady also believed in this, and her struggle to go there was described in that novel. In the story there was also a young orphan girl who falls in love but there was no money for the wedding. In the end, the old lady gives away all her savings without going to Kashi. She says, 'The happiness of this orphan girl is more important than worshipping Lord Vishweshwara at Kashi.' My grandmother, Krishtakka, never went to school so she could not read. Every Wednesday the magazine would come and I would read the next episode of this story to her. During that time she would forget all her work and listen with the greatest concentration. Later, she could repeat the entire text by heart. My grandmother too never went to Kashi, and she identified herself with the novel's protagonist. So more than anybody else she was the one most interested in knowing what happened next in the story and used to insist that I read the serial out to her. After hearing what happened next in Kashi Yatre, she would join her friends at the temple courtyard where we children would also gather to play hide and seek. She would discuss the latest episode with her friends. At that time, I never understood why there was so much of debate about the story. Once I went for a wedding with my cousins to the neighbouring village. In those days, a wedding was a great event. We children enjoyed ourselves thoroughly. We would eat and play endlessly, savouring the freedom because all the elders were busy. I went for a couple of days but ended up staying there for a week. When I came back to my village, I saw my grandmother in tears. I was surprised, for I had never seen her cry even in the most difficult situations. What had happened? I was worried. 'Avva, is everything all right? Are you ok?' I used to call her Avva, which means mother in the Kannada spoken in north Karnataka. She nodded but did not reply. I did not understand and forgot about it. In the night, after dinner, we were sleeping in the open terrace of the house. It was a summer night and there was a full moon. Avva came and sat next to me. Her affectionate hands touched my forehead. I realized she wanted to speak. I asked her, 'What is the matter?' 'When I was a young girl I lost my mother. There was nobody to look after and guide me. My father was a busy man and got married again. In those days people never considered education essential for girls, so I never went to school. I got married very young and had children. I became very busy. Later I had grandchildren and always felt so much happiness in cooking and feeding all of you. At times I used to regret not going to school, so I made sure that my children and grandchildren studied well ...' I could not understand why my sixty-two-year-old grandmother was telling me, a twelve-year-old, the story of her life in the middle of the night. But I knew I loved her immensely and there had to be some reason why she was talking to me. I looked at her face. It was unhappy and her eyes were filled with tears. She was a good-looking lady who was usually always smiling. Even today I cannot forget the worried expression on her face. I leaned forward and held her hand. 'Avva, don't cry. What is the matter? Can I help you in any way?' 'Yes, I need your help. You know when you were away, Karmaveera came as usual. I opened the magazine. I saw the picture that accompanies the story of Kashi Yatre and I could not understand anything that was written. Many times I rubbed my hands over the pages wishing they could understand what was written. But I knew it was not possible. If only I was educated enough. I waited eagerly for you to return. I felt you would come early and read for me. I even thought of going to the village and asking you to read for me. I could have asked somebody in this village but I was too embarrassed to do so. I felt so very dependent and helpless. We are well-off, but what use is money when I cannot be independent?' I did not know what to answer. Avva continued. 'I have decided I want to learn the Kannada alphabets from tomorrow onwards. I will work very hard. I will keep Saraswati Pooja day during Dassara as the deadline. That day I should be able to read a novel on my own. I want to be independent.' I saw the determination on her face. Yet I laughed at her. 'Avva, at this age of sixty-two you want to learn alphabets? All your hair are grey, your hands are wrinkled, you wear spectacles and you work so much in the kitchen...' Childishly I made fun of the old lady. But she just smiled. 'For a good cause if you are determined, you can overcome any obstacle. I will work harder than anybody but I will do it. For learning there is no age bar.' The next day onwards I started my tuition. Avva was a wonderful student. The amount of homework she did was amazing. She would read, repeat, write and recite. I was her only teacher and she was my first student. Little did I know then that one day I would become a teacher in Computer Science and teach hundreds of students. The Dassara festival came as usual. Secretly I bought Kashi Yatre which had been published as a novel by that time. My grandmother called me to the puja place and made me sit down on a stool. She gave me a gift of a frock material. Then she did something unusual. She bent down and touched my feet. I was surprised and taken aback. Elders never touch the feet of youngsters. We have always touched the feet of God, elders and teachers. We consider that as a mark of respect. It is a great tradition but today the reverse had happened. It was not correct. She said, 'I am touching the feet of a teacher, not my grand daughter; a teacher who taught me so well, with so much of affection that I can read any novel confidently in such a short period. Now I am independent. It is my duty to respect a teacher. Is it not written in our scriptures that a teacher should be respected, irrespective of the gender and age?' I did return namaskara to her by touching her feet and gave my gift to my first student. She opened it and read immediately the title Kashi Yatre by Triveni and the publisher's name. I knew then that my student had passed with flying colours.

EXERCISE

"I could not understand why my sixty-two-year-old grandmother was telling me, a twelve-year-old, the story of her life in the middle of the night. But I knew I loved her immensely and there had to be some reason why she was talking to me."

The heart warming story of the bond between a granddaughter and her grandmother is sure to bring nostalgic memories of grandparents to everyone who reads it. The cherished memories of the author is a story worth treasuring as it is set in the rich Indian cultural context imparting the value of love and respect towards elders and the message that learning has no boundaries of age and it is timeless.

A. Write your opinion about how to treat grandparents and state the reasons following the guidelines given below:

- Title
- Opening Statement
- Analysis
- Argument
- Evidence
- Conclusion

Build your opinion using these phrases: First of all, ... I believe that, … In addition, …, I think, … In my opinion … Nowadays, … In fact, … I disagree that, … In conclusion, …

B. Resume

Here is a basic resume template:

- Contact Information:
  - Name
  - Address
  - Phone Number
  - Email
  - LinkedIn Profile (or other relevant social media)
- Summary/Objective:
  - Brief overview of your experience, skills, and career goals (optional)
- Education:
  - Degree, Field of Study, University, Graduation Date
  - Relevant courses, academic achievements, or honors
- Work Experience:
  - Job Title, Company, Employment Dates
  - Brief description of job responsibilities and achievements
  - Quantifiable results and accomplishments (e.g., "Increased sales by 25% in 6 months")
- Skills:
  - Technical skills (e.g., programming languages, software proficiency)
  - Soft skills (e.g., communication, teamwork, leadership)
- Achievements/Awards:
  - Relevant awards, certifications, or publications

- Volunteer/Relevant Extracurricular Activities:
  - Brief description of relevant volunteer or extracurricular activities
- **References:**
  - Available upon request (or include 2-3 professional references)

Task: Draft your resume to apply in a prestigious company.